CQ's White House Media Simulation

CQ's White House Media Simulation

Government in Action

Julie Dolan
Macalester College

and

Marni Ezra
Hood College

CQ PRESS

A Division of Congressional Quarterly Inc.
Washington, D.C.

CQ Press
A Division of Congressional Quarterly Inc.
1255 22nd Street, N.W., Suite 400
Washington, D.C. 20037

202-822-1475; 800-638-1710

www.cqpress.com

♾ The paper used in this publication meets the minimum requirements of the American National Standard for Information Sciences—Permanence of Paper for Printed Library Materials, ANSI Z39.48-1992.

Cover and interior designs: Karen Doody

Printed and bound in the United States of America

05   04   03   02   01   5   4   3   2   1

Library of Congress Cataloging-in-Publication Data
In process
   ISBN 1-56802-711-7

To Our Parents

Contents

Foreword

CQ Press is pleased to introduce a new line of educational tools designed to incorporate traditionally researched topics into a learning environment. The long-awaited Government in Action series offers firsthand experience on the workings of the government. Whether read in the library by patrons interested in learning about the government or used in the classroom by students and instructors, the Government in Action series is a rich classroom-tested tool that will benefit anyone seeking to gain a better understanding of how our democracy works. Volumes in the series include *CQ's Legislative Simulation: Government in Action, CQ's White House Media Simulation: Government in Action, CQ's Congressional Election Simulation: Government in Action,* and *CQ's Supreme Court Simulation: Government in Action.*

To enhance the simulation experience, a free instructor's manual on how to conduct a classroom simulation is offered on the Web at http://library.cqpress.com/gia. Whether encouraging library research or conducting classroom simulations, the Government in Action series is an ideal reference tool. We are very interested in your impression of our new series, and we encourage you to send your feedback to GIAFeedback@cqpress.com.

CQ Press

Preface

The relationship between the president and the White House press corps has long been a favorite subject for study by academics and others, including members of the press. Although citizens learn about this relationship from reading press accounts and observing White House briefings, speeches, and other events, and students learn about it in their political science classes, neither group can experience the White House press operation first-hand because of the difficulty of visiting the White House and observing the daily interaction among the president, his staff, and the press.

The purpose of this book is to provide readers with opportunities to play roles in three events that occur frequently in the White House—two, in fact, on a daily basis. They are the daily gaggle, in which reporters meet briefly in the morning with the press secretary to get a heads-up on the president's day; the press secretary's daily afternoon briefing with reporters; and a presidential address in the White House Rose Garden, an event the president uses occasionally to put forth his views on a particular issue. We have used simulations extensively in our courses, and they have been highly regarded by our students, who consistently report that the simulations bring to life the course material.

Organization of the Book

This book is divided into two parts. In Part I, Chapter 1 serves as a primer on the White House press operation and the White House press corps. We suggest that participants read this chapter before starting the simulation. Chapter 2, a guide to the simulation itself, walks participants step by step through the exercise and their roles and responsibilities in it.

Part II provides some of the supporting materials on the two substantive issues we selected as a focus for the White House staff and the press in the simulation—faith-based and community initiatives and U.S.-China relations. The materials include background articles and any laws or regulations governing the issue under discussion. Although participants in the simulation will need to use outside sources to research their own roles, all the information they will need on the issues is included in Part II.

Acknowledgments

Many people gave us their helpful comments and support in getting this book published. First, we would like to thank our editor at CQ Press, Adrian Forman, for overseeing this project from beginning to end, and Sabra Bissette Ledent for her insightful and helpful editing. We also are indebted to several people in the White House press corps who opened their minds and schedules to us so that we could observe them in action. In particular, Naftali Bendavid of the *Chicago Tribune* and Edwin Chen of the *Los Angeles Times* answered endless questions and provided us with valuable insights. Mimi Hall of *USA Today* allowed us to use her pool report. We also want to thank the members of the White House Press Office who provided much useful information. In addition, we are grateful to our student assistants, Megan Mills and Julie Fouché, who reviewed the manuscript and provided us with helpful comments.

Julie Dolan
Marni Ezra

A White House Media Primer

CHAPTER 1

The White House and the Media

To have an effective presidency, [Gerald Ford's chief of staff Richard] Cheney reminded me, the White House must control the agenda. An essential element of that control, he explained, is the ability to maintain discipline within the administration itself. Any appearance of disunity among the president's ranks will be seized upon by the media as an opportunity for a story—one that will undermine the president's agenda.

—John Anthony Maltese, *Spin Control:*
The White House Office of Communications and
the Management of Presidential News, 1994

The White House Press Corps gathers every morning like a pride of lions. It snarls and growls, sleeps and creeps, and occasionally loves, but it is always hungry.
—Marlin Fitzwater, *Call the Briefing:*
Bush and Reagan, Sam and Helen: A Decade with
Presidents and the Press, 1995

As the only nationally elected leader in the United States, the president is responsible for keeping Americans informed about what he is doing on their behalf.[1] In communicating with the American public, the president uses many different avenues: weekly radio addresses, State of the Union messages, press conferences, and even the White House Web site. In these instances, the president speaks directly to the people and retains control of the information and message conveyed. Yet because he does not use these means frequently enough to keep the public totally informed and in touch with the White House, the president also must rely on members of the press to communicate his messages and accomplishments to the public.

The president and the White House press corps have always had a close yet adversarial relationship.[2] As described later in this chapter, within the White House the president and his staff work in close proximity to the press corps—only a few corridors and closely guarded doors away. Located between the West Wing and the rest of the White House, the White House press quarters contain working space for reporters and a room used for press briefings. Reporters learn almost immediately when something newsworthy has occurred and quickly press the administration for information. In doing its job, the press reports the news with the ultimate goal of selling newspapers or gaining viewers. It is not the goal of the press to serve the White House, to make the president look good, or to give the president time to come up with a response to a difficult situation. On the other hand, the president and the White House communications team want to make the administration look as good as possible while they toil away in behalf of the American public. But sometimes presenting the administration's best face means withholding information or framing an issue in a way that helps the president's case or even spinning information in a certain direction. In seeking to be fair-minded, the press will attempt to remove the spin presented by the administration and report the news as neutrally as possible.

Because the goals of the press corps and the White House differ, tension often arises between the two as they try to influence each other. Some scholars have suggested that the White House press corps and the president have a symbiotic relationship that sometimes turns adversarial.[3] The relationship is symbiotic in that each group works in close proximity to the other and the two groups need each other. The press corps relies on the president to provide the news it needs to fill its daily news and feature stories, and the president relies on the press corps to transmit his ideas and messages to the American public. The relationship sometimes turns adversarial, however, because each group often has divergent goals and perspectives. Presidents prefer to be covered in as positive a light as possible, but such coverage does not always translate into lively, newsworthy stories. The Clinton White House even relied on punitive sanctions to respond to individual journalists who published particularly negative news stories about the administration. According to *Washington Post* media reporter Howard Kurtz, "If you ticked off your White House handlers, they might not return your calls or give you much information, and you would be stranded."[4] Earlier, during the Johnson administration, LBJ thought CBS was "out to get us," so Johnson's White House refused to grant the network any favors or special access.[5]

This chapter examines the roles and responsibilities of the White House staff members who work to facilitate relations between the president and the White House press corps. The two primary offices entrusted with developing and managing communications strategy for the president are the White House Press Office and the White House Office of Communications, which over the years has gone by many names. In addition, the chapter provides a brief history of presidents' relationships with the press and identifies some of the tactics commonly used by administrations in trying to secure positive press coverage of the president. Finally, the chapter describes the goals, responsibilities, and perspectives of the White House press corps.

History of the White House Press Operation

Article II of the Constitution specifies that the president "shall take Care that the Laws be faithfully executed." Despite the vagueness of the wording, most scholars agree that it provides the president with the power to preside over the many cabinet departments and agencies that constitute the vast federal bureaucracy. However, the president cannot undertake such an enormous task by himself. He is assisted by a cabinet composed of the heads of the various executive branch departments such as Defense, State, and Health and Human Services and also receives assistance from a variety of staff members employed within the Executive Office of the President (EOP). In recent years, the EOP has been made up of some ten offices and councils, including the White House Office (WHO), the Office of Management and Budget (OMB), and the National Security Council (NSC).

Not all presidents have enjoyed such assistance, however. In fact, Franklin D. Roosevelt, who served from 1933 to 1945, was the first president to benefit from the services of more than a handful of personal presidential aides.[6] In response to the Great Depression of the 1930s, the federal government created scores of agencies and commissions

to implement and execute FDR's New Deal programs passed by Congress. In 1936, President Roosevelt appointed the Committee on Administrative Management, more popularly known as the Brownlow Committee, to recommend a strategy for reorganizing the growing federal bureaucracy.[7] The committee recommended that the president receive some help in coordinating and managing the executive branch and that the new aides not be subject to confirmation by the Senate, in contrast with the standard procedure for other presidential appointments such as cabinet secretaries.[8] This recommendation was passed into law several years later as part of the Reorganization Plan of 1939, which allowed the president to hire six personal assistants to carry out "such duties as the president may prescribe."[9] The White House staff is much larger today, made up of approximately 450 staffers who serve at the pleasure of the president.[10] The president's communications and press staffs, which fall into this category, work in the White House Office, which is located physically within the West Wing of the White House. They are commonly referred to as part of the White House staff.

In the early days of the United States, presidents did not require the assistance of a press staff; rather, they dealt personally with the reporters who covered them. In fact, it was not until President William McKinley took office in 1897 that a president designated someone to carry out the duties of the modern press secretary.[11] (Before then, presidents had generally relied on their private secretaries not only to tend to administrative matters but also to provide the press with information and facilitate news-gathering arrangements.) Indeed, McKinley is widely credited with making use of the first presidential press secretary, although the position was not called that for several years. He appointed George B. Cortelyou as his confidential stenographer, and Cortelyou proceeded to take on the responsibilities of modern press secretaries, such as briefing reporters, writing and distributing press releases, and even providing advance copies of presidential speeches to members of the press.[12] Since Cortelyou's days, all presidents have employed press secretaries to assist them in their relations with the media.

The relationship between the president and the press in those days was much more simple and straightforward than it is today. McKinley's successor, President Theodore Roosevelt, held his own informal press conferences in the White House.[13] Such events were possible at the time because only a handful of reporters covered the White House. Outside the White House, the president rarely communicated with the American people in the way that presidents do today. Because there was no television or radio, presidents typically waited until the State of the Union address to speak to the nation. Aside from that, they communicated with the public only when a constitutional question arose, and those addresses were infrequent. In fact, throughout most of the nineteenth century political reporters and the general public were more interested in the happenings at the other end of Pennsylvania Avenue, where Congress was busily carrying out its constitutional duties.[14] It is only relatively recently that the press has decided to devote more resources to covering activities in the Oval Office.

Since those earlier days, relations between the president and the press corps have greatly changed. For one thing, the White House press corps is much larger, making it impossible for the president to engage in the same type of freewheeling exchange with members of the media that was once possible. Because the demand for news about the president has not lessened, the president today employs a staff of about fifty to package, distribute, and transmit newsworthy information to the media, including the press secretary, the director of communications, and their staff members.[15] The next section details the roles and responsibilities of the White House press operation.

Roles and Responsibilities of the Presidential Communications Staff

The president relies chiefly on the Office of Communications and the White House Press Office to manage his administration's dealings with the media. The press secretary presides over the Press Office and usually reports to the head of the Office of Communications, typically referred to as the director of communications.[16] Both of these officials, who are appointed by the president, are high-ranking presidential advisers and trusted confidantes of the president. For example, Press Secretary Ari Fleischer and counselor to the president Karen Hughes in the George W. Bush administration both worked on Bush's presidential campaign. Likewise, during Bill Clinton's first administration, Dee Dee Myers and George Stephanopoulos served as press secretary and director of communications, respectively, positions they were appointed to after working on Clinton's 1992 campaign (see Table 1 for a list of press secretaries and communications directors who have served since the Nixon administration).

Both the press secretary and director of communications share responsibility for acting as liaison between the president and the White House press corps, and much of their

Table 1 Recent Press Secretaries and Directors of Communications

President	Press Secretary	Director of Communications
Richard Nixon	Ronald Ziegler	Herbert Klein
		Ken Clawson
Gerald Ford	Jerald terHorst	Paul Miltich/James Holland[a]
	Ron Nessen	Gerald Warren[a]
		Margita White[a]
		David Gergen
Jimmy Carter	Jody Powell	Gerald Rafshoon
Ronald Reagan	James Brady	Frank Ursomarso
	Larry Speakes	David Gergen
	Marlin Fitzwater	Michael McManus
		Pat Buchanan
		John Koehler
		Thomas Griscom
		Mari Maseng
George Bush	Marlin Fitzwater	David Demarest
		Margaret Tutwiler
Bill Clinton	Dee Dee Myers	George Stephanopoulos
	Michael McCurry	Mike Gearan
	Joe Lockhart	Don Baer
		Ann Lewis
		Loretta Ucelli
George W. Bush	Ari Fleischer	Dan Bartlett

Sources: Michael J. Towle, "In Behalf of the President: Four Factors Affecting the Success of the Presidential Press Secretary," *Presidential Studies Quarterly*, 27, no. 2 (1997): 297–319; Washington Monitor, *Federal Yellow Book* (Washington, D.C.: Washington Monitor, 1995–2000); and John Anthony Maltese, *Spin Control: The White House Office of Communications and the Management of Presidential News*, 2d ed. (Chapel Hill: University of North Carolina Press, 1994).

[a] The Nixon administration's Office of Communications was involved in the Watergate affair. Upon assuming office after Nixon's resignation, President Gerald Ford initially decided not to establish a White House Office of Communications. As such, the responsibilities usually assigned to this office were subsumed under the duties of the Press Office and continued as such until David Gergen took over as head of the new Office of Communications in July 1976.

jobs require figuring out how to communicate the president's desires and actions to the press so that this information will ultimately reach its intended audience, the U.S. public. Both strive to achieve positive coverage of the president's agenda, policy priorities, speeches, and daily activities and to deflect any negative coverage. Indeed, as one scholar put it, "The chief job of presidential press officers is precisely to obtain positive news slant and deflect negative."[17]

Although the two offices work toward the same purpose—securing positive media coverage for their boss—they often do so in slightly different ways. In general, the press secretary is more intimately engaged with news reporters, serving as the presidential mouthpiece every day of the week. In describing his role, former Clinton press secretary Joe Lockhart explained, "I see myself as someone who believes in what the president is doing, and a good part of my job is finding ways to articulate it."[18] In contrast, the communications director focuses on long-range planning and figuring out how to set the agenda, stage events, and engage in other activities that will likely produce positive press coverage. As John Maltese explains the difference between the two, the Press Office is concerned primarily with providing information for the White House itself and "seldom moves beyond the short-term goal of disseminating the news of the day and responding to reporters' queries"—that is, "the Press Office is primarily reactive and the Office of Communications is primarily proactive."[19]

The Director of Communications

As noted, the director of communications focuses on managing and staging the news, doing whatever it takes to achieve positive media coverage by developing a long-term perspective and communications strategy and thinking carefully about how each presidential event will appear on the news. According to Maltese, "the modern presidency is much like an ongoing political campaign. As in any campaign, the president must set the agenda, maintain discipline among his spokespeople, and orchestrate media coverage of that agenda through long-term public relations planning."[20] The communications director is at the forefront of these efforts.

The president necessarily relies on the press to communicate with the American public, but presidents usually prefer to go directly to the American public without having to pass through the filter of the media. John F. Kennedy was the first president to televise his press conferences, which allowed him to speak directly to the public without being subjected to the media's editing and filtering.[21] Indeed, Samuel Kernell has detailed the efforts of many modern presidents to "go public"—that is, to take their message directly to the American public via televised press conferences, prime-time addresses to the nation, well-placed speeches before various groups, and White House ceremonies.[22] The intended effect of going public, and therefore bypassing the power of journalists and media organizations to report only that part of the presidential message *they* think is newsworthy, is to persuade the public of the righteousness of the president's message and encourage citizens to place pressure on their members of Congress to go along with whatever the president

advocates. In doing so, the president hopes to bypass the media, thereby controlling the agenda and the message.

The president's communications staff prefers to leave little to chance when it comes to conveying presidential messages, and so often attempt to manipulate the media in ways that increase their chances of getting a certain message across. As veteran communications director David Gergen explained, "We had a rule in the Nixon operation . . . that before any public event was put on his [the president's] schedule, you had to know what the headline out of that event was going to be, what the picture was going to be, and what the lead paragraph would be."[23] Although presidential appearances may appear spontaneous and unscripted on the news, the communications staff carefully selects which presidential events are open to the media and then stages them to increase the probability of receiving positive coverage. The communications director maintains frequent contact with members of the press, but for the purpose of spinning and controlling the news, not for simply passing along information from the administration.

One of the most useful tactics favored by the Office of Communications in its efforts to control the media is the "line-of-the-day," a sentence or phrase that is repeated ad nauseum throughout the day by all administration officials in an attempt to coax the press into focusing on the president's agenda. Michael Deaver, President Ronald Reagan's communications director, once explained that repetition is a key component of managing the media. If all administration officials repeat the line-of-the-day over and over, the theory is that the press will eventually absorb the message, increasing the probability that the president's unedited and unfiltered words will find their way into journalists' stories.[24]

The communications staff also employs a variety of other tactics to ensure that the president receives positive media coverage. One of these tactics is to spin the news, to "scrub it of dark scandal stains, remove unsightly splotches of controversy, erase greasy dabs of contradictions, and present it to the country crisp and sparkling white."[25] The essence of "spin control" is to take a piece of potentially damaging information or news and tweak it so that the president ends up looking good. Strategies for spinning the news to reflect positively on the president include dispatching administration officials to speak on behalf of the president on the Sunday morning television news shows such as NBC's *Meet the Press,* submitting positive editorial pieces to the major national newspapers (or encouraging others to do so), using the line-of-the-day to ensure that all administration officials are speaking from the same script, and bypassing the national media outlets by going directly to local newspapers and media organizations, which are usually less cynical and skeptical about the information they receive from the presidential establishment.[26]

President Ronald Reagan and his staff were masters at manipulating the media, figuring out what kinds of stories the press would run with and crafting them to ensure maximum positive impact for the president.[27] An oft-cited example illustrates the point. As CBS reporter Lesley Stahl tells the story, she had written a negative piece attacking Reagan's tendency to gloss over unpopular policy positions by saturating the television airwaves with glowing images of the president. To accompany her story, she assembled a variety of these previously aired video clips to illustrate that Reagan's policy actions did not always comport with the images portrayed on television, hoping to reinforce her point that the president often said one thing but did quite another. For example, although Reagan had cut housing budgets for the elderly, he was shown cutting the ribbon at an old folks' home. Stahl thought her piece would infuriate the president's communications staff and so was quite surprised to receive an enthusiastic phone call from an administration official telling her how great the piece was. As she paraphrases him, he reminded her that "when you're showing four and a half minutes of great pictures of Ronald Reagan, no one listens to what you say. . . . The public sees those pictures and they block your message. They didn't even hear what you said. So, in our minds, it was a four-and-a-half minute free ad for the Ronald Reagan campaign for reelection."[28] The lesson learned is that knowing that visual coverage predominates when combined with audio coverage, and so the president's communications staff thinks carefully about how to assemble visually appealing images to accompany presidential appearances.

As its name implies, the Communications Office is also entrusted with the job of coordinating the news flow from the entire executive branch. Each of the cabinet-level departments and many executive agencies has its own press operations, and the White House Office of Communications keeps in touch with these offices, coordinating their messages in order to minimize the possibility that contradictory statements might emerge from different sources.[29] Although this coordination may seem a simple task, the vast size of the federal bureaucracy—over two million government workers—requires careful management and control efforts so that each organization understands and promotes the White House agenda. In undertaking this job, the Office of Communications relies on the line-of-the-day to facilitate projecting a unified presidential administration to members of the media.

In summary, today's presidents rely heavily on their communications staff to communicate their actions and policy priorities to the American public. In that communication, the press secretary is perhaps the most visual figure, because he or she is responsible for disseminating the president's message, which is filtered through the White House press corps. The role and responsibilities of the White House press secretary are described in the next section.

The Press Secretary

The three primary responsibilities of the press secretary are to serve as chief liaison between the president and members of the press, to work in conjunction with other communications staff members in the White House to achieve positive media coverage and deflect the negative, and to advise the president on communications matters.

Scholar Michael Towle has emphasized how important it is for the press secretary, as the liaison between the press and the president, to maintain good working relationships with both.[30] Indeed, having the respect of one or the other but not both does not bode well for a press secretary. If he or she has the confidence of the president but not of the press, the members of the press will treat him or her with skepticism and often disregard the information provided, convinced they are being fed the administration line. A press secretary who enjoys the confidence of the press corps but not the president risks being left out of the loop by the president and therefore is of questionable use to the members of the media. Dee Dee Myers, President Clinton's first press secretary, was viewed as ineffective primarily because she had insufficient access to the president.[31]

But as Michael McCurry, President Clinton's second press secretary, has suggested, maintaining the confidence of the White House press corps is not always easy. As the chief spokesperson for the president, the press secretary's words are treated as official White House pronouncements and highly scrutinized by the media, who often search for any inconsistencies with previously released administration information. Thus if McCurry made any mistake, even "if he was off by a micro-faction," he might be "denounced as venal and corrupt and a liar" by members of the press.[32] Moreover, under such circumstances his relations with individual members of the press corps might be tarnished, even if he had not deliberately misled them. On the other hand, as McCurry lamented, members of the press could make a major mistake in one of their stories and never offer any apology for or acknowledgement of their error. True, they would run or air a correction, but it was likely to be buried in some obscure part of the paper or appended to the end of a related on-air news story.

As described in more detail in the next section, part of the press secretary's liaison responsibility is carried out through two specific meetings between him or her and the White House press corps. The first, the "gaggle," is the more informal of these meetings, and it usually takes place in the morning in the press secretary's office. The second, the afternoon press briefing, is an opportunity for the press secretary to make official pronouncements about presidential actions and positions and to answer reporters' questions. These briefings are televised by C-SPAN, a practice begun by Clinton press secretary Michael McCurry.[33] The Office of the Press Secretary also provides reporters with written transcripts of the daily news briefings,[34] disseminates press releases when necessary (see box "Samples, White House Press Releases"), and engages in various other duties that keep the press corps up-to-date on the activities and priorities of the president.

To be effective, a press secretary must have open channels of communication with the president, at least to some degree, in order to be able to pass on whatever information the president and his advisers deem important. The press secretary also needs to anticipate the kinds of questions reporters are likely to ask so he or she can consult with the president and other communications staff members and draft appropriate responses ahead of time. As McCurry explained, the job of the press secretary consists of "telling the truth, giving the people a window on the White House, and protecting the president."[35]

Protecting the president while also telling the truth sometimes requires that the press secretary leave some questions unanswered, especially if the answers jeopardize national security or refute previous statements made by the administration. While serving as Clinton's press secretary, McCurry explained that he would not always ask the president for information on everything the press was likely to inquire about. If he did and the president relayed damaging information, he would either have to lie to the press if the question was raised or transmit the damaging material. During the impeachment proceedings, by remaining out of the loop and passing the reporters off to Clinton's lawyers, McCurry was able to answer honestly that he did not have the information they sought and remain fairly confident that the president's lawyers would

honor attorney-client privilege and keep the information to themselves.[36]

In addition to serving as a conduit between the media and the president, the press secretary plays an advisory role to the president. One means of advising the president is the pre-brief, a session the press secretary holds with the president and other senior advisers such as the communications director to prepare the president for any questions he might face when the press is within shouting distance.[37] Although members of the press often complain that they do not have enough access to the president, members of the presidential communications staff prefer to keep it that way in order to minimize any embarrassing comments the president may utter unwittingly.[38]

But who exactly are these members of the press, and what are their perspectives on the difficult job of covering the most powerful man in the world? The next section describes the makeup and function of the White House press corps.

The White House Press Corps

From its vantage point close to the Oval Office, the White House press corps reports on every aspect of the presidency, both personal and political. Laboring in close quarters and under tight deadlines, the press corps frames and often shapes the way in which the president is presented to citizens of the United States and to the world. This section details the workings of the White House press corps, including its history, its organization, and its relationship to the president and his staff.

The Correspondents

Though the numbers vary slightly from year to year, approximately one hundred reporters cover the White House on a regular basis. Many more, however, are members of the accredited White House press corps. Some seventeen hundred reporters are issued a press pass which they receive once they are accredited and have received clearance from both the White House and the Secret Service. Many well-known journalists such as Sam Donaldson, Wolf Blitzer, Helen Thomas, Andrea Mitchell, Dan Rather, and Eleanor Clift served as White House correspondents. After all, the White House beat is one of the most prestigious in Washington.

Most major newspapers such as the *New York Times, Los Angeles Times,* and *Washington Post* have at least one full-time White House correspondent. In addition, the wire services,

SAMPLE WHITE HOUSE PRESS RELEASES

THE WHITE HOUSE
Office of the Press Secretary

FOR IMMEDIATE RELEASE   March 14, 2001

President George W. Bush today announced his intention to nominate four individuals to serve in his administration.

The President intends to nominate William Burns to be Assistant Secretary of State for the Near East. He is a career Foreign Service Officer who has held the post of Ambassador to Jordan since 1998 and served as Special Assistant to the President and Senior Director for the Near East and South Asian Affairs from 1986 to 1989. He is the recipient of a number of State Department awards including the Distinguished Honor Award and the James Clement Dunn Award.

The President intends to nominate Lou Gallegos to be Assistant Secretary of Agriculture for Administration. He currently serves as Chief of Staff to Governor Gary Johnson of New Mexico and has served as the Secretary of the New Mexico Human Services Department. In 1989 he was appointed Assistant Secretary of the Interior for Policy Management and Budget. He is a veteran of the U.S. Air Force and a graduate of New Mexico Highlands University.

The President intends to nominate Powell A. Moore to be Assistant Secretary of Defense for Legislative Affairs. He currently is Chief of Staff for Senator Fred Thompson of Tennessee. He was appointed Assistant Secretary of State for Intergovernmental and Legislative Affairs in 1982 and served former President Reagan as Deputy Assistant to the President for Legislative Affairs in 1981. Originally from Millegville, Georgia, Moore is a veteran of the U.S. Army and a graduate of the University of Georgia.

The President intends to nominate John Charles Weicher to be Assistant Secretary of Housing and Urban Development and serve as the Federal Housing Commissioner. He is presently a Senior Fellow and Director of Urban Studies at the Hudson Institute and serves as Assistant Secretary for Policy Development and Research from 1989 to 1993. He was Associate Director of Economic Policy at the Office of Management and Budget from 1987 to 1989 and was Deputy Assistant Secretary for Economic Affairs at HUD from 1975 to 1977. He is a graduate of the University of Michigan and received his Ph.D. from the University of Chicago.

THE WHITE HOUSE
Office of the Press Secretary

FOR IMMEDIATE RELEASE   March 14, 2001

President George W. Bush today announced his intention to nominate Richard J. Egan to be Ambassador Extraordinary and Plenipotentiary of the United States to Ireland.

"The United States and Ireland enjoy natural bonds of friendship and strong trade and investment relationships. I am pleased to announce my intention to nominate Dick Egan as Ambassador to Ireland as I prepare to meet with Prime Minister Ahern and celebrate St. Patrick's Day and the rich heritage of the Irish people. Dick Egan has experienced extraordinary success in the private sector and has a broad-based background. He is an ideal person to serve as Ambassador to Ireland as we look forward to working even more closely with our Irish friends," said President Bush.

Mr. Egan is the founder and current director of EMC Corporation in Hopkinton, Massachusetts, and established the Hopkinton Technology for Education Foundation. He is a veteran of the Unites States Marine Corps and a graduate of Northeastern University.

which are large news organizations that cover a wide range of news topics and then sell their stories to news outlets that do not have their own correspondent in a certain news area, also are represented in the press corps. For example, the *Frederick News-Post* in Frederick, Maryland, which does not have a White House correspondent, relies on the wire services, such as the Associated Press (AP), United Press International (UPI), or Reuters, for its coverage of the White House. Newspapers that purchase the wire services often alter the wire story to make it more interesting for their readers. Finally, the major television and cable networks such as CNN, ABC, CBS, and NBC, radio stations such as National Public Radio, and periodicals such as *Time* and *Newsweek* are also represented in the press corps.

Some of the major newspapers represented in the White House press corps have two full-time journalists who divide their time between daily and feature stories. Daily stories cover the president's daily activities and the current White House events. The reporters who write daily stories may attend White House events on a given day, including the gaggle and the briefing. Feature stories typically cover a specific topic or person and may require days or weeks to produce or write. For example, prior to the 2000 presidential election the *Washington Post* ran a series of feature stories about each presidential candidate.

The Press "Pools"

The entire press corps, however, does not always cover the president. At many events both inside and outside the White House, such as a presidential Rose Garden address, the entire press corps is invited to attend. But when the event is too small for all reporters to be present, as many are, a small number of members of the press corps are selected to attend the event based on the "pool rotation." The idea of pool reporting originated in the cold war era when the press wanted to keep a twenty-four-hour body watch on the president because he held the keys to the nuclear codes. So that all members of the press did not have to stay up all night, the press rotated its coverage and took turns following the president's every move.

There are two types of press "pools": the in-town pool and the travel pool. The in-town press pool consists of representatives of the news organizations that cover the White House on a regular basis, and the thirteen members of the pool change each day and rotate alphabetically. For example, approximately twenty-nine print media organizations, nine radio organizations, five television networks,

and three periodicals are represented in the White House press corps.[39] Thus each day some, but not all, of the organizations from each type of media cover the pool events—that is, those events that the White House specifies can only be attended by the reporters in the daily pool (see box "News Organizations Represented in the White House Press Pool"). The second type of pool, the travel pool, accompanies the president when he travels on Air Force One, flying alongside him while the rest of the reporters travel in a separate press plane.

In both types of pools, each reporter from each respective type of media organization then reports back to the members who were not part of that day's pool. For example, the representative of the print press in the pool has the responsibility for writing a pool report that all of the other reporters can use for their stories (see box "Sample Pool Report"). In the pool report the journalist, among other things, describes the event, provides the appropriate quotes, and assesses the president's and other officials' moods.[40] Although the print reporter has the advantage of being able to ask questions directed at a particular story of interest to him or her, pool reporters must follow two rules. First, they must file their reports before writing their own stories. Second, they may not use anything in their own stories that was not put in the pool report. These rules protect the rest of the press corps from receiving only partial information and makes for a more collegial group.

The White House Briefing Room and Press Quarters

The White House press corps works in a low-level building that links the West Wing, occupied by the president and his staff, to the rest of the White House. This building consists of three areas in which the press spends most of its time—the upper press office, the lower press office, and the briefing room (see box "White House Briefing Room and Press Quarters"). The "upper press office" is not really an office at all but a small open area outside the press secretary's office where the press occasionally gathers. On the first day of the Clinton administration, in a move that infuriated the White House press corps, the upper press office was closed to reporters for the first time. The press felt closed off from the press secretary, unable to gain proper access.[41] The decision was almost immediately reversed, because "the symbolism of that act, and the practicality of it, deeply offended the White House Press Corps."[42] Moreover, the banishment, dubbed "an act of war" by veteran UPI correspondent Helen Thomas, ensured a rough

NEWS ORGANIZATIONS REPRESENTED IN THE WHITE HOUSE PRESS POOL (2001)

Print

Austin American Statesman
Baltimore Sun
Boston Globe
Chicago Tribune
Christian Science Monitor
Columbia Dispatch
Copley Newspapers
Cox Newspapers
Dallas Morning News
Gannett Newspapers
Hearst Newspapers
Knight Ridder
Los Angeles Times
McClatchy
McClendon
Media General
Newhouse
Newsday
New York Daily News
New York Post
New York Times
Pittsburgh Post Gazette
Scripps Howard
St. Louis Post-Dispatch
United Press International (UPI)
USA Today
Wall Street Journal
Washington Post
Washington Times

Radio

ABC
American Urban
Associated Press (AP)
Bloomberg
CBS

National Public Radio
SRN
Talk Radio
Voice of America

Television

ABC
CBS
CNN
Fox
NBC

Periodicals

Newsweek
Time
U.S. News and World Report

Wire Services / Wire Photo / Agency Photo

Agence France Presse
Associated Press (AP)
Bloomberg
Newsmakers
Reuters

Example of a Daily Pool

On March 15, 2001, the daily pool was composed of:

Wires: AP, Reuters, Bloomberg
Wire photo: Agence France Press, AP, Reuters
TV correspondents and crew: CBS
Lights: CNN
Magazine photo: *Newsweek*
Radio: AP
Print: *Washington Post*
Agency photo: Newsmakers

beginning to relations between the press and the Clinton White House.

A few steps and a short corridor connect the upper press office to the briefing room where the press gathers each day for the afternoon briefing with the press secretary. The briefing room is smaller and more crowded than it appears on television; it has only forty-eight seats which are assigned to reporters from the different news organizations. In past administrations, as either a punishment or a perk to reporters seen as antagonistic or friendly, the press secretary would assign good or bad seating to certain members of the press corps. Today, however, the seats are permanently assigned—the front rows to the major networks, wire services, and the most prestigious newspapers such as the *New York Times* and *Washington Post*. Visitors and members of the press who are not assigned a

SAMPLE POOL REPORT

Pool Report No. 1
Flight to NJ, Grace Episcopal Church
Uneventful flight to New Jersey. No one came back to the press cabin to brief.
Joining POTUS on AFONE:
White House staffers Joe Hagin, Nick Calio, Scott McClellan, Dan Bartlett
Sen. Bob Toricelli
Sen. Jon Corzine
Rep. Rodney Frelinghuysen
Rep. Mike Ferguson
Rep. Rush Holt (the only Democrat)
Rep. Frank LoBiondo
Rep. Jim Saxton
Rep. Chris Smith
Rep. Marge Roukema

At the airport, POTUS was greeted by: Gov. and Mrs. Donald diFrancesco, Speaker Jack Collins, the Hon. Rev. DeForest Soaries, Jr. (the NJ Secretary of State, also known as "Buster.")
Rabbi Allen Silverstein
Rev. Tae Ho Ahn
Bishop Paul Bootkoski, the interim leader of the Archdiocese of Newark

POTUS took Marine One for a 20-minute ride to Plainfield, followed by a 5-minute motorcade to Grace Episcopal Church, a small red brick church in a low-income neighborhood. There, he was escorted into the basement, a large tan and off-white painted cinderblock room used for the Youth Entertainment Academy, a faith-based after-school program run by the Plainfield Interfaith Neighborhood Council for Housing.

He took a little tour around the edges of the room and greeted several students there to show him their activities. He also took several questions from the pool on the stock market, carbon dioxide and his faith-based initiative. You'll have a transcript.

First, Tiffany Tate, 12, and Jordanne Cox, 11, showed POTUS their computer. Their conversation with him was out of earshot of your pool but we did hear POTUS tell one of the girls, "You don't look nervous."
Next, several high school boys showed POTUS their band equipment (drums, a keyboard and some mikes) and played several songs for him.

Mark Cox, a man who appeared to be the director of the program (we were not told of his title) guided much of the tour. He told POTUS that the program was funded for 20 kids but they now have 43 on the roster.

POTUS spoke of "an Army of compassion in America" and said he was there to highlight that. He urged Congress to fund faith-based programs but added, "Government cannot make people love each other. I wish we could." (please see transcript)

One of the program administrators, a woman named Angela, described to POTUS how the teachers provide home-cooked meals for the kids on Mondays. She said she teaches the kids etiquette and POTUS seemed to appreciate that, offering a hearty nod.

POTUS proceeded to the side of the room where the band equipment was set up.
Raheem Morsan, the drummer, asked POTUS if he plays any instruments.
"No," was the reply.
When someone suggested that Morsan could teach POTUS how to play, POTUS responded, "You better be a heck of a teacher."

Morsan: "What kind of music do you like?"
POTUS: "You name it."

The band then played a soft gospel song while POTUS sat to the side on speaker. The band has two singers, a drummer and keyboard player.

After the song, POTUS and the drummer had a conversation, only part of which was audible, about choices and priorities.

Morsan noted that the after school program "is good for me because it keeps me occupied. I could be out doing a lot of things."

POTUS suggested that Morsan should pass on what he's learned to younger kids. Morsan replied: "My mom, she's always telling me to pass it on to my little brother."

POTUS: "That's good. There you go."

The band then played Amazing Grace. "That's one of my favorites," POTUS said.

Rev. La Verne Ball, president of the Plainfield Interfaith Neighborhood for Housing (but NOT the pastor of Grace church), then told POTUS how grateful she was that he's come to the program. An aside: After she was done speaking, the cell phone in her pocket went off. But POTUS didn't react.

POTUS responded: "I can't thank you all enough for providing a little haven of love and support."

He added, "We ought to welcome faith-based programs into our society not fear them." (please check against transcript)

One banner in the room read: "Your attitude can make a difference."

A welcome banner read: "President George W. Bush—Welcome to Plainfield."

Finally, POTUS took questions from the pool. Here are a few quotes:

On the turmoil in the markets: "I'm concerned that a lot of Americans' portfolios have been affected. . . . But I've got great faith in our economy."

On the reversal of his campaign promise on carbon dioxide: "We're in an energy crisis now." (this is something he repeated three times)

"Ours is an administration that will deal with the problems of the day."

"I was responding to the reality—and the reality is the nation has a real problem when it comes to energy."

On his faith-based legislation: "We're moving on a timetable that we're comfortable with."

"We will move our package and I'm confident it will get passed."

"I'll be signing a good bill."

Mimi Hall/USA TODAY

permanent seat in the briefing room stand in the side aisles to observe or ask questions. The members of the foreign press who are frequently present may ask the press secretary questions which may focus on their respective countries or regions.

In the front of the briefing room is a small stage furnished with a podium bearing the presidential seal and a microphone; a blue curtain forms the backdrop. The secretary conducts the briefing from the podium. To the press secretary's right are four seats reserved for the secretary's deputies or other administration officials on hand to assist the secretary with the briefing if called upon. Television

cameras are set up in the rear of the briefing room, and roving camera operators move about the room, coming within feet of the press secretary.

At the back of the briefing room is a short, narrow hallway that connects the briefing room to the lower press office where members of the press are assigned small cubicles in which to work. "Each of the networks has a booth not much bigger than a walk-in closet in the back of this room. Inside, there is a counter with typewriters, a television set, and several phone lines—little else."[43] The atmosphere in the press room is informal. Most reporters are dressed casually and are engaged, when not working,

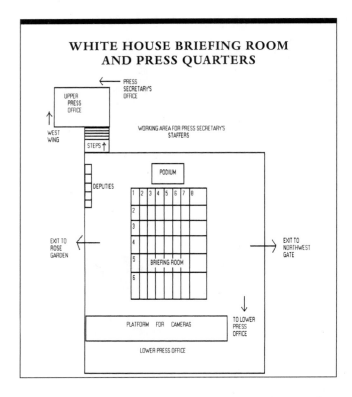

WHITE HOUSE BRIEFING ROOM AND PRESS QUARTERS

in a multitude of activities, including eating lunch, playing cards, reading, or napping. There is nothing casual, however, about the reporters' quest for information, which is the focus of their daily activities.

A Day in the Life of a White House Reporter

Members of the White House press corps cover the White House from early in the morning until late at night. Their days are only as predictable as the activities of the president. If the president suddenly decides to travel or deviate from his daily schedule, the press corps must adjust its schedule accordingly.

Prior to the Reagan administration, the press secretary would brief the press twice a day, once in the morning and once in the afternoon. In the early 1980s, the morning briefing was replaced with an informal meeting with reporters that eventually became dubbed the "gaggle" during the Clinton administration.

Early in the morning, the press secretary's staff notifies the press corps via beeper or e-mail about the gathering time for the morning "gaggle." It typically begins between nine and ten in the morning and lasts fifteen to twenty minutes. The press waits outside the door of the press secretary's office until he or she opens it and invites them in. Although the gaggle is "on the record" (a term explained shortly) and is recorded by many reporters, no cameras are allowed (see box "Sample Transcript, White House Press Gaggle").

The number of reporters attending the gaggle varies. If reporters have a specific question or piece of information they want to confirm, they will attend; otherwise, they may wait for the afternoon briefing. The gaggle is especially important for the wire services. Because the wires have ongoing deadlines to meet throughout the day, the gaggle provides them with information early in the news cycle.

At the gaggle, members of the press huddle around the press secretary's desk and turn on their tape recorders. After copies of the president's daily schedule, at least the public one, are distributed, the press secretary details each appearance that the president will make on that particular day and explains the role the press will have in these events (see box "Sample Press Schedule of the President's Day"). For example, the schedule for March 15, 2001 (see box), explains that the pool will accompany the president in a motorcade to the Capitol. When the Friends of Ireland luncheon begins, the pool will be present. The reference to "Pool at Top" means the in-town pool of reporters will be ushered into the event at the beginning (or the top) so that they can briefly take pictures and ask a few questions. Then they are ushered out.

After reviewing the schedule, the press secretary opens the floor for questions from the press. Often, substantive matters discussed at the gaggle come up again at the afternoon briefing. The give-and-take between the reporters and the press secretary may be laced with good humor— or the atmosphere may be contentious.

The gaggle benefits both reporters and the press secretary. The press gets to ask questions, listen to the press secretary, "soak and poke" around the West Wing, and attempt to talk to other administration officials who might assist them with their stories. The press secretary is able to assess the mood of the press, determine what they want to hear about that day, and better prepare for questions that might come up at the afternoon briefing.

After the gaggle, reporters typically go back to their cubicles in the lower press room or to their offices outside of the White House to work on the stories they will write that day. Because of the cramped White House quarters, many reporters prefer to work in their news offices. As Mara Liasson, a reporter for National Public Radio, describes her White House "office," "If I stick out my elbows in both directions I can touch either wall."[44]

In addition, the press corps (or depending on the event, just the press pool) attends the events on the president's public schedule such as presidential addresses, photo opportunities, or talks to constituent groups. At these events, the press is sometimes able to question senior administration officials and staffers about the event itself or gather infor-

SAMPLE TRANSCRIPT, WHITE HOUSE PRESS GAGGLE

The following excerpt is from Press Secretary Ari Fleischer's January 22, 2001, gaggle with the White House press corps. Complete transcripts can be read online at http://www.whitehouse.gov/news.

10:02 a.m. EST

MR. FLEISCHER: . . .Okay, let me go over the President's schedule for the day, a couple of other things. He arrived at 7:20 a.m., into the Oval Office. He had a security briefing; met with the Chief of Staff. Of course, you just saw this morning, he had the staff—I'm not sure how Karl Rove got in there. He's meeting with the Secretary of State at 10:00 a.m.; then he's got some other meetings, focus on personnel.

He will have lunch this afternoon with GOP House and Senate leaders. And let me, on that, give you—the attendees are Trent Lott, Senator Don Nickles, Senator Rick Santorum, Senator Larry Craig, Senator Kay Bailey Hutchison, Senator Bill Frist, Speaker Dennis Hastert, Majority Leader Dick Armey, Majority Whip Tom DeLay, Conference Chairman J.C. Watts, Policy Committee Chairman Chris Cox, Vice Chairwomen of the Republican Conference Deborah Pryce, Secretary of the Republican Conference Barbara Cubin, Chairman of the NRCC Tom Davis, Chief Deputy Majority Roy Blunt and Congressman Rob Portman, who is the Chairman of the Elected Leadership Group, they have set that back up again in the House.

Q: What time?

MR. FLEISCHER: That meeting is at noon.

Q: Where is it?

MR. FLEISCHER: That meeting is the Old Family Dining Room. If any of you could tell me where that is, I'd be obliged. (Laughter.)

Q: Upstairs.

MR. FLEISCHER: Then at 1:00 p.m. he has a—

Q: Do you expect people from that lunch to come talk with us afterwards?

MR. FLEISCHER: Oh, I'm sure they—do I expect members of Congress to go to a microphone after a meeting? (Laughter.)

Q: Like a heat-seeking missile. (Laughter.)

Q: The first dumb question—(Laughter.)

MR. FLEISCHER: Well, I've never worked there; I don't know what they do. (Laughter.)

Then at 1:00 p.m. he has a Successful Reading Providers meeting, which I think is going to be a rather interesting meeting. And the purpose of it is, there are a whole series of things that the President-elect discussed at great length in the campaign, that he thinks are going to be profound at changing education. That's what this is all about. I won't belabor that point right now, but it's really going to get into the substance of how do you change education so teachers know how to teach children to read.

And when it comes to education reform, I know there's a lot of focus on vouchers and other more controversial issues—to him, this and standards are the core of how do you actually help children to read. There are a whole series of other important issues, but reading—he's called it net civil right, he's talked about making sure every child can read by 3rd grade. That's why this is his first meeting on his first day of the presidency.

Q: Is the First Lady involved in that, at all?

MR. FLEISCHER: Let me see if she's attending.

Q: How about his mom?

MR. FLEISCHER: No, I think they're out of town. I don't have that—we'll have the list of attendees. It's a lot of teachers, it's a lot of academics, it's a lot of professors. We have a particular cache in the skills of teaching reading. It's from the education community; it's just a real who's who list.

Other events, since we're reading. Then he will meet this afternoon with a group of very senior Democratic Party officials.

Q: Who are they?

Q: Why? What are their names?

MR. FLEISCHER: Ambassador Robert Strauss, Dick Moe, Jody Powell, Bill Gray III, Senator Paul Simon, Senator John Glenn. And the purpose of the meeting is two-fold.

One is, as the sign of the seriousness which President Bush takes for achieving bipartisan consensus in this town, and say, get used to it. He is going to continue to identify those Democrats who will be most willing to work with him.

Q: They aren't in office.

MR. FLEISCHER: Pardon me?

Q: —retired, these people don't have the inside power.

MR. FLEISCHER: I think they have a little bit to do with—a little bit. There are people on the Hill he's going to continue to meet with, of course. But these people could play instrumental roles still. And he also specifically asked them today for their help in getting these education reforms back to pass on the Hill.

Q: Ari, is he looking for his Washington version of Bob Bullock?

MR. FLEISCHER: I don't think he would put it in those terms. I'm not sure he would put it that way. Bob Bullock was unique. Bob Bullock was unique in terms of the power he had—and by definition of the powers of Lieutenant Governor of Texas and the relationship they established. So I don't think he can recreate him. But he's going to look for lots of ways to reach out to Democrats.

Q: Ari, what, precisely, is he going to ask this group to do and what can they do, given the fact that they're all retired?

MR. FLEISCHER: Well, they talk to Democrats on the Hill all the time. They help set the tone, they help change the tone in Washington. These are people who are known for the goodwill, their ability to work well with the other party. And the reaching out to the Democrats is going to be an ongoing priority of the President.

And like I say, there are going to be some who will work with him; others will simply choose not to, out of ideology. We will continue every effort to find those who will work with us and grow that list and do more with them.

Q: —identify any that are in office right now?

MR. FLEISCHER: Well, they're coming up. The Democrats are coming up. We have a bipartisan meeting tomorrow. So get used to it. There will be lots of meetings.

Q: The question is getting used to—we're not used to this kind of—you know, these people coming into power—has-beens and so forth—have they given a commitment to the President on the education problem and are they for vouchers?

MR. FLEISCHER: I think we'll hear from them later.

Q: But why were they picked in that respect?

MR. FLEISCHER: Because the President views them as senior statesmen who came to Washington for a considerable period of time and who have an interest in helping to govern, not just oppose.

Q: —forum in this kind of an ongoing dialogue with the elected Democratic leadership?

MR. FLEISCHER: Oh, he will. But they're coming tomorrow. And he's met with many of them already. So you saw that on our services committee, you saw that on education. So it's part of the pattern.

Q: Ari, Zell Miller is cosponsor of the tax—this morning. What's the President's response to—

MR. FLEISCHER: Okay, let me get to one file, a logistical piece that you all need to know.

Q: Can we just ask logistics about that last thing? What's the coverage of the meeting, itself?

MR. FLEISCHER: We should have all this in writing, it should have been distributed in writing. Not there?

The Dem meeting at the end of the day is pool at the top; in the Cabinet Room, pool at the top.

Q: What time?

Q: The reading?

MR. FLEISCHER: The reading is pool at the end, Roosevelt Room. That will be approximately 1:00 p.m.—the end of that meeting is approximately 1:50 p.m, that's the reading initiative. And the Democrat leaders is pool at the top, 3:40 p.m. in the Cabinet Room.

One final piece, and that is President Bush will travel to San Cristobal, Mexico, on February 16th, to meet with his Excellency Vincente Fox, President of the United Mexican States. The meeting will be an opportunity to begin the process of achieving closer ties between the United States and Mexico and expanding areas of cooperation. . . .

THE PRESS: Thank you.

END 10:20 a.m. EST

SAMPLE PRESS SCHEDULE OF THE PRESIDENT'S DAY

THE WHITE HOUSE

The Office of the Press Secretary

FOR PLANNING PURPOSES ONLY   March 14, 2001

PRESS SCHEDULE OF THE PRESIDENT FOR THURSDAY, MARCH 15, 2001

<u>Intown Travel Pool:</u>

Wires: AP, Reuters, Bloomberg
Wire Photo: AFP, AP, Reuters
TV Corr & Crew: CBS
Lights: CNN
Mag Photo: Newsweek
Radio: AP
Print: Washington Post
Agency Photo: Newsmakers

8:30 am   Intown Travel Pool gathers in the Brady Press Briefing Room

11:50 am   THE PRESIDENT departs The White House en route US Capitol

               POOL accompanies in motorcade

11:55 am   THE PRESIDENT arrives the US Capitol

12:05 pm   THE PRESIDENT participates in Friends of Ireland Luncheon

               Capitol Building

               POOL AT TOP

1:55 pm   THE PRESIDENT departs The Capitol en route The White House

               POOL accompanies in motorcade

2:00 pm   THE PRESIDENT arrives The White House

THERE ARE NO OTHER PUBLIC EVENTS ON THE PRESIDENT'S SCHEDULE FOR MARCH 15, 2001

Note: **9:30 am Gaggle in the Press Secretary's Office**
             2:30 pm Briefing by the Press Secretary in the Brady Press Briefing Room

---

mation about another story that they are writing (see next section). The nature of the event and the president's mood determine whether he will answer the press's questions.

The next major interaction between the press and the press secretary is the daily afternoon briefing. The briefing usually takes place in the White House briefing room between twelve and two in the afternoon, depending on the president's and press secretary's schedules. But some re-porters may choose not to attend. Unlike in the 1980s when the press flocked to the briefings, today reporters may rely instead on the transcript of the briefing, which is available almost immediately and sent to the press via e-mail (see box "Sample Transcript, White House Daily Briefing").[45]

At the briefing, the press secretary may begin with a statement or simply take questions from the press corps. Because briefings usually last no longer than a half-hour,

SAMPLE TRANSCRIPT, WHITE HOUSE DAILY BRIEFING

The following excerpt is from Press Secretary Ari Fleischer's February 1, 2001, briefing with the White House press corps. Complete transcripts can be read online at http://www.whitehouse.gov/news/briefings/.

1:50 p.m. EST

Q: Ari, a question about the disability event today. Has the President expressed any concern about the Americans with Disabilities Act's impact on small businesses or on proliferation of sometimes frivolous lawsuits? And is there anything in the initiative that would modify the ADA in any way?

MR. FLEISCHER: Well, in terms of modify the ADA, it's a proposal to add on to the ADA. And so the answer to that is yes, in that sense. I have not heard the President address it in any other manner than what he described today and what he described during the campaign.

Q: On the theme of bipartisanship, is the President inclined to let Democratic U.S. Attorneys fill out their terms, especially in places like New York, where there's some precedent for that?

MR. FLEISCHER: Let me see what we're doing with the U.S. Attorneys. Let me take that and get back to you.

Q: February 1st, Black History Month.

MR. FLEISCHER: Yes.

Q: President Bush is talking about inclusion, healing, civil rights are cornerstone of his administration. Is he going to celebrate Black History Month in a way of bringing initiatives and things of that nature?

MR. FLEISCHER: A proclamation is in the works and as soon as it is done and final we will issue it and have it for you.

Q: Will John Ashcroft be part of that?

MR. FLEISCHER: I have not read the language of the proclamation.

Q: President Clinton is giving an interview to Israeli TV at a very delicate juncture in both Israeli politics and the peace process. Does the President believe that's helpful?

MR. FLEISCHER: I haven't discussed it with him.

Q: Ari, you said, by definition the Ashcroft vote would be bipartisan. But also, by any mathematics, it is the least bipartisan of all of the confirmation votes. What does it say to you about the ability of this administration to communicate to Democrats its message about a controversial nominee and their ability to respond?

MR. FLEISCHER: I've been in this town a long time and I've seen a lot of votes in the Senate that had a small number of members of the opposite party vote with someone, and those have been labeled bipartisan in the past. So I think that same standard ought to apply here.

Q: Why—in the past or now?

MR. FLEISCHER: Because I think it's accurate.

Q: It's accurate, but—

Q: On the congressional retreats, how did the invitations to the Democratic retreats come about?

MR. FLEISCHER: It was kind of a mutual thing. The President let it be known that he would be willing to go, and he was invited.

Q: Will he also be taking questions at the retreat in addition to just providing prepared remarks? A couple House members said they thought it was sort of a condition of him coming, that they would be able to ask him policy questions—

MR. FLEISCHER: Tradition of him coming? Presidents—

Q: No, no, an expectation of him coming.

MR. FLEISCHER: Oh.

Q: They would want the opportunity and the opportunity would be provided for them to ask questions of the President.

MR. FLEISCHER: I haven't looked at the agenda in that detail. I'll be there tomorrow.

Q: Would that surprise you?

MR. FLEISCHER: I'll be there, and so I'll find out.

Q: There are reports that former President Clinton is going to Israel a couple of days before the election. Does the White House think that is a proper role for him to be playing?

MR. FLEISCHER: I'd refer you to State as far as that goes.

Q: You don't have an opinion? You don't know whether or not he is—

MR. FLEISCHER: It's not been a topic of discussion.

Q: —getting involved in their election?

MR. FLEISCHER: It's not been a topic of any discussions that I've been involved in.

Q: Can you take the question?

MR. FLEISCHER: Let me see what I can do on that one, Ron.

Q: Has the President done away with the playing of "Hail to the Chief," at routine events? Does he have a policy—

MR. FLEISCHER: No, he has not gotten rid of that. It will be played—I think it will just be played at fewer occasions rather than more occasions, but it will, indeed, be played.

Q: Does he not like the song, or what's the—

MR. FLEISCHER: He likes the song a whole lot, as a matter of fact. He worked hard to get it played. But it will be played, just not at every occasion.

Q: Why?

Q: How does he decide?

MR. FLEISCHER: For example, there are some events that—in our first week, the room was filled up and we didn't have a band in there. There will be other occasions where we will and we'll have it played. There's really no rhyme or reason. It's just going to be an occasional thing.

Q: Has it been played at any events, Ari, as far as you know?

MR. FLEISCHER: I don't think. Not yet.

Q: Has he hummed it or whistled it on the way in—(laughter.)

MR. FLEISCHER: I don't know when he left campus—on the occasions when I was with him when he did, I didn't hear it played—humming and whistling—

Q: But why—

MR. FLEISCHER: I don't know.

Q: Did he dance to it?

MR. FLEISCHER: He box-stepped to it.

Q: Why on fewer occasions? Was it used too much under Clinton and you want to save it for—

MR. FLEISCHER: No. Like I said, I think there's really no fancy rhyme or reason to it.

Q: Ari, you have one Democrat in the Cabinet, Norman Mineta. Are there any other Democrats in consideration, say, for example, the U.N., or some of the other jobs that are still out there?

MR. FLEISCHER: Well, of course, you notice that the person the President chose to head his faith-based office is a Democrat. As any other announcements get made, we will report them and you'll be able to evaluate at that time.

Q: Is the President going to be paying any special attention to the Israeli election as far as monitoring it, and if he is, in what way? And did he ever mention of any special preference that he has in the outcome?

MR. FLEISCHER: The President, of course, is aware of this election, but he's not going to involve himself in any way.

Q: He has never said any preference, like who he'd rather have—

Q: Ari, at the prayer meeting this morning, did he have any contact, interaction with other foreign leaders?

MR. FLEISCHER: I asked that, and I'm advised, no.

Q: You were going to give us a week ahead, since you're not going to be here tomorrow.

MR. FLEISCHER: I'm not prepared to do that today. What I'm going to do is try to do that with the pool, and then you'll get the pool report. It will be a week ahead from Williamsburg.

Q: Do you know what the themes will be here, just in general, next week?

MR. FLEISCHER: Taxes. Taxes and budget.

Q: If tomorrow morning's event at the Library of Congress is such an extraordinary occasion, why is it closed? Why is the coverage closed?

MR. FLEISCHER: Retreats are traditionally closed events.

Q: Except for Williamsburg, which is open.

MR. FLEISCHER: That's an unusual event.

Q: Ari, what about the radio address? Is that going to be live or is he going to tape it?

MR. FLEISCHER: It will be taped.

Q: With enough time ahead of time to have a transcript?

MR. FLEISCHER: I'd like to, if I can.

Q: Is he still going to Camp David Friday night?

MR. FLEISCHER: Yes, he is.

END 2:15 P.M. EST

each reporter is not always able to ask a question. Members of the press resort to all kinds of strategic methods in attempting to get called on; they raise their hands, gesture, speak loudly, and call out the press secretary's name in an attempt to get recognized. The closer reporters sit to the press secretary, the better their chances for recognition. Often in response to a certain question, the press secretary will simply refuse to answer and move on to the next one. At other times, the press secretary will provide detailed, colorful answers. Meanwhile, reporters seek to update information they received at the gaggle and obtain from the press secretary confirmation of or details about information harvested elsewhere.

The atmosphere during the briefing depends greatly on two things. The first is the relationship between the press and the press secretary. During some administrations and during the tenure of certain press secretaries, the relationship has been tense. For example, as noted, the press did not trust Dee Dee Myers, Clinton's first press secretary, because they thought she did not have enough access to President Clinton and therefore they could not trust her answers.[46] The second factor is the nature of the daily news. On an ordinary day the mood is more casual. On a day where there is something that the White House wants to keep from the press, whether a new legislative proposal, foreign mission, or scandal, the press will endlessly hound the press secretary into answering their questions. In 1998, when President Clinton's alleged affair with White House intern Monica Lewinsky was in the headlines, Press Secretary Michael McCurry told the press that Clinton had denied that he had had "any improper relationship" with Lewinsky. The press, however, would not accept the prepared statement given to McCurry and questioned him so persistently that, in frustration, he responded to a question by NBC's David Bloom by saying, "I'm not leaving any impression, David, and don't twist my words."[47]

If the issue of concern to the press on a certain day is highly technical or complex, an expert may be brought in to provide additional information. For example, if the president goes on a foreign trip the national security adviser may walk the press through the president's schedule and the agenda. Such briefings are either on the record or are attributed to a senior administration official. If the president is meeting with foreign leaders, a staff member provides the press with a summary of the meeting as soon as it is over, or the press secretary will provide the summary during the regular briefing. If the president spent the morning on Capitol Hill meeting with congressional leaders, the afternoon briefing might focus on those meetings. After the afternoon briefing, the reporters continue to work on their stories, calling sources, checking facts, and pursuing new leads. They must meet evening deadlines, either in the form of appearances on the networks' nightly news shows or filing stories for the next day's newspaper edition. Network reporters make sure they have the right footage or photos for their news stories and incorporate the information acquired throughout the day's events into their narratives.

News Gathering

In the White House itself, reporters are limited in their news gathering because their physical access to administration officials with offices in the West Wing is extremely limited. The press area is closed off from the rest of the White House by the door outside of the upper press office. Reporters are permitted to roam in the small area outside of the press secretary's office (the upper press office), where they may wait for officials to pass in and out of that office, but they may not follow them into the West Wing. Reporters may attempt to ask officials questions, but the officials may or may not answer, depending on their mood. As for encounters with the president, as veteran reporter Helen Thomas notes, "If one of the White House press-office people comes by and says the President's going jogging, you drop everything, grab your notebook, get your coat, and start running."[48]

Members of the press can obtain an interview with a White House official in one of two ways. A reporter can go through the White House Press Office, which will contact the official the reporter wants to interview and then inform the reporter whether the individual will agree to be interviewed. Or the reporter can call the official directly to set up an interview or work through the press secretary for a particular office. The method used depends on the official being interviewed. Some like to have their offices handle requests, and some prefer to have requests handled through the press office.

When a reporter is trying to interview other sources, such as members of Congress and lobbyists, they call the source's office, explain what they are writing about, and ask for an interview. Success in getting an interview hinges on many factors, including the persistence of the reporter, the prestige of the reporter's news outlet (for example, a *Washington Post* reporter may have more success than one representing a lesser-known newspaper), the prestige of the person being sought for an interview, the topic of the story, and whether or not the potential interviewee feels it is important to state his or her point of view. Obtaining sources willing to discuss many sides of an issue is crucial to reporters.

Once an individual has agreed to an interview, the information that emerges can be attributed in several ways: on the record, on background, on deep background, and off the record. Most reporters prefer to report information that is *on the record*—that is, the source agrees to associate his or her name with the information reported. Journalists prefer this type of disclosure because it gives the reported information more legitimacy.

Many times, however, sources do not want to be named. Fearing retribution or embarrassment, they may insist that the reporter refrain from using descriptors in the story that would identify them as the source. When this is the case, the interview is conducted *on background* and the reporter negotiates with the source how the information will be attributed. Often a source who is unwilling to be named directly will agree to be referred to as "a senior administration official" or "an individual close to the story."

The third category of attribution is *deep background*. At times, a source does not want any attribution but will allow the information provided to be used in the story. In this case, the reporter obliges by using the information but not disclosing any source.

Some sources may agree to give a reporter information provided that the reporter makes no mention—either directly or indirectly—of the information they provided. The information provided *off the record* may help the reporter to better understand a story or issue or will lead the reporter to other sources of information.

Conversations with sources are assumed to be on the record unless the source says otherwise. The general rule is to establish the attribution guidelines up front so there is no confusion. It is possible that part of an interview can be given on the record and that at a certain point the source will ask for the interview to be off the record or on background. As for those sources revealing information on background, on deep background, and off the record, reporters are bound to protect their identity—in fact, reporters consider it a sacred duty. After all, reporters must rely on their own good reputation for confidentiality to gain future leads.

Finally, when writing a story reporters do not go to each other for information. The competition for exclusives and the pressure among newspapers, networks, and periodicals is so fierce and relentless that reporters must rely on their own initiative and ingenuity to gather reliable sources of up-to-date information.

Changes in Press Coverage of the White House in the 1990s

In his important work *Feeding the Beast*, Kenneth Walsh, a former member of the White House press corps, details some changes in the way the press has covered the White House over the last decade.[49] A sign that the presidency was declining in importance as a source of news was the reduced commitment by the press corps during the Clinton administration to maintain the twenty-four-hour "body watch" that developed during the cold war. Reporters who missed the Kennedy assassination because they decided to relax and have a drink spent the rest of their careers regretting their decision. Today, journalists claim that intense coverage of the president is not as critical as in earlier days. With modern technology, they do not need a pool report for an important event because they are able to watch the event on television.

Another factor that has influenced the way the White House press corps covers the president is the escalating cost of covering the president on the road.[50] Many news sources have severely cut back on their coverage, and others, mostly smaller news organizations, have been priced out of covering the president altogether. Because the press pays for all of its own travel, covering the president can be an extremely expensive proposition. In November 1994, President Clinton announced he would go to Budapest to sign several nuclear nonproliferation agreements and discuss security concerns with the country's European allies. For the press, the opportunity to take a few nice photos was outweighed by the cost of the trip, which would exceed $10,000 per person. Deterred by the high price tag, many journalists backed out. For the remaining interested reporters, the cost of chartering a plane for the event became prohibitive, because it could no longer be split among many news organizations.

Finally, yet another factor that changed coverage of the presidency in the 1990s was the decision-making styles of the Clintons and the Clinton administration and their attitude toward the press. The Clinton administration often made decisions at the last minute, leaving the press scrambling to arrange travel and accommodations and meet other types of deadlines.[51] In addition, Clinton and his staff were consistently late, especially frustrating members of the press with tight deadlines, and officials in the Office of Communications frequently kept members of the press waiting at length for interviews that at times failed to materialize.

This chapter has described the critical roles played by both the White House communications staff and the White House press corps in framing the news that Americans watch and read about their president. Chapter 2 will take you through the simulation process itself, reviewing the roles to be played in the three parts of the simulation and the responsibilities that accompany those roles.

Notes

1. Throughout U.S. history, all presidents have been men. Thus we use the word he to refer to those who have already served in the office, not to suggest that only men can hold the position.
2. We would like to thank Naftali Bendavid, national correspondent for the *Chicago Tribune,* and Edwin Chen, national correspondent for the *Los Angeles Times,* for providing much of the background information for this chapter. They were very generous in detailing their careers as White House reporters for us.
3. Samuel Kernell, *Going Public: New Strategies of Presidential Leadership,* 3d ed. (Washington, D.C.: CQ Press, 1997); and Mark J. Rozell, "The Press and the Presidency," in *Understanding the Presidency,* ed. James P. Pfiffner and Roger H. Davidson (New York: Longman, 1997).
4. Howard Kurtz, *How the White House and the Media Manipulate the News* (New York: Touchstone, 1998), 39.
5. Quoted in Michael Baruch Grossman and Martha Joynt Kumar, "The White House and the News Media: The Phases of Their Relationship," *Political Science Quarterly* 94, no. 1 (1979): 37–53.
6. John P. Burke, *The Institutional Presidency* (Baltimore: Johns Hopkins University Press, 1992).

7. Ibid., and James P. Pfiffner, *The Modern Presidency* (New York: St. Martin's Press, 1994).
8. These appointments do not require Senate confirmation so that the president receives the greatest latitude in choosing his closest advisers. See President's Committee on Administrative Management, *Reorganization of the Executive Departments* (Washington, D.C.: Government Printing Office, 1937).
9. Reorganization Act of 1939, Title III, Section 301.
10. James P. Pfiffner, "Executive Office of the President," in *A Historical Guide to the U.S. Government,* ed. George T. Kurian (New York: Oxford University Press, 1998). See *U.S. Government Policy and Supporting Positions,* also known as the *Plum Book,* for a list of these positions <www.access.gpo.gov/plumbook/2000/toc.html>.
11. W. Dale Nelson, *Who Speaks for the President? The White House Press Secretary from Cleveland to Clinton* (Syracuse, N.Y.: Syracuse University Press, 1998).
12. Ibid., 16.
13. Ibid.; and Rozell, "The Press and the Presidency," 88–99.
14. Kernell, *Going Public*; and Nelson, *Who Speaks for the President?*
15. Washington Monitor, *Federal Yellow Book* (Washington, D.C.: Washington Monitor, 1995–2000).
16. In the George W. Bush administration, the Press Office reports to Karen Hughes whose official title is Counselor to the President, Strategic Planning, Communications, and Speechwriting. Bush has chosen a model in which there is no Office of Communications as such. Martha Joynt Kumar, personal communication, August 22, 2001.
17. Robert M. Entman, *Democracy without Citizens: Media and the Decay of American Politics* (New York: Oxford University Press, 1989), 65.
18. Dana Milbank, "White House Watch: Joe Cool," *New Republic,* March 1, 1999, 14.
19. John Anthony Maltese, *Spin Control: The White House Office of Communications and the Management of Presidential News,* 2d ed. (Chapel Hill: University of North Carolina Press, 1994), 5.
20. Ibid., 150.
21. Kernell, *Going Public,* 86.
22. Ibid.
23. Quoted in Hedrick Smith, *The Power Game: How Washington Works* (New York: Ballantine Books, 1988), 401.
24. Mark Hertsgaard, *On Bended Knee: The Press and the Reagan Presidency* (New York: Farrar Straus Giroux, 1988).
25. Kurtz, *How the White House and the Media Manipulate the News,* xv–xvi.
26. Maltese, *Spin Control*; and Hertsgaard, *On Bended Knee.*

27. Hertsgaard, *On Bended Knee.*

28. Quoted in Smith, *Power Game,* 409.

29. Maltese, *Spin Control.*

30. Michael J. Towle, "On Behalf of the President: Four Factors Affecting the Success of the Presidential Press Secretary," *Presidential Studies Quarterly,* vol. 27, no. 2 (1997): 297–319.

31. Kurtz, *How the White House and the Media Manipulate the News.*

32. Ibid., 157.

33. Ibid., 17. C-SPAN routinely covers the daily press briefing and provides actual video coverage of recent briefings on its Web site <www.c-span.org/executive/briefings.asp>.

34. Also available on the Web <www.whitehouse.gov/news/briefings>.

35. Kurtz, *How the White House and the Media Manipulate the News,* 15.

36. Ibid.

37. Ibid., 64.

38. Hertsgaard, *On Bended Knee.*

39. The size of the press corps varies, as does the representation in the press pool. For example, before the George W. Bush administration, Bush's home state newspaper, the *Austin American Statesman* was not in the pool rotation but an Arkansas paper was.

40. Naftali Bendavid, national correspondent, *Chicago Tribune,* interview by Marni Ezra, February 15, 2001. As explained by *Newsweek*'s Martha Brandt,

    While most of the press corps slept in last Thursday, Ed Chen of the *Los Angeles Times* was at the Crawford Elementary School by 5:15 a.m. President [George W.] Bush was going golfing, and Chen had drawn the short straw: he was on "pool duty." Every time the president goes anywhere publicly, the press goes too. The group of thirteen—photographers, camera and sound men, and reporters representing newswires, radio, TV, newspapers and magazines—becomes the eyes and ears for the rest of the press corps.

    Quoted in Howard Kurtz, "Media Becomes the Bad News Bears," *Washington Post,* August 31, 2001.

41. Kenneth T. Walsh, *Feeding the Beast* (New York: Random House, 1996), 127.

42. Edwin Chen, national correspondent for the *Los Angeles Times,* interview by Marni Ezra, February 20, 2001.

43. Frederic T. Smoller, *The Six O'Clock Presidency* (New York: Praeger, 1990).

44. Sarah Jones, "Mara Liasson Is NPR's Window to the White House," March/April 2000 <www.herald-sun.com/listen/magz/0300/030006.html>, accessed August 24, 2001.

45. Transcripts of daily briefings are online <www.whitehouse.gov/news/briefings>.

46. Walsh, *Feeding the Beast.*

47. Howard Kurtz, *Spin Cycle: Inside the Clinton Propaganda Machine (New York: Free Press, 1998), xi.*

48. Walsh, *Feeding the Beast,* 265.

49. Ibid.

50. Ibid.

51. The White House Travel Office makes the logistical arrangements for the press on all presidential trips, including a charter plane, lodging, food, ground transportation, and equipment. As noted, the costs of press travel are shared by the news organizations attending an event.

CHAPTER 2

Guide to the Simulation

The process by which the White House communicates its message and the press corps interprets that message for the American public can be tense at times. As the president tries to put the administration's best side forward to the citizens, the press may uncover or interpret the administration's words or actions in a less-favorable light. Many books have been written about the White House and the media organizations that cover the president, but it is hard to understand this relationship without actually experiencing it. The purpose of this simulation is to provide a firsthand understanding of the complex relationship between the White House communications operation and the White House press corps and the ways in which they interact on a daily basis. It also provides participants with insight into how the White House press corps, Office of Communications, and Press Office work and the ways in which the White House attempts to craft and deliver its message to the public through the press.

How the Simulation Works

This simulation places you, the participant, in the center of a presidential speech in the White House Rose Garden and within two press events—the early morning gaggle in the press secretary's office and the afternoon press briefing—that occur on a daily basis in the White House. You will participate in one, two, or all three events, depending on your role. If you are playing the president, you will participate only in the Rose Garden speech and the press conference that follows; if you are playing a member of the White House press corps, you will participate in all three events. But no matter what your role, you are encouraged to undertake all the research needed to carry out your role as realistically as possible.

The simulation takes place, for the most part, in real time—that is, all of the events that occur on or around the period of time the simulation is played out are those that will provide its context. Participants are encouraged to read the newspapers and watch television news on a daily basis to know what issues of importance the administration is considering. If the most important news during the week of the simulation is the midterm congressional elections, a legislative proposal on carbon dioxide emissions, or air strikes against a foreign nation, these events should be covered by the press within the simulation.

Along with such real news events, the simulation deals with two issues that are described briefly later in this chapter and in Part II: faith-based and community initiatives, a proposal put forth by the Republican presidential candidate, George W. Bush, in the 2000 election campaign, and U.S.-China relations. Although the main issue in the simulation may not be featured prominently in the news when you conduct the simulation, you should pretend that the issue is currently on the administration's front burner. For example, human rights issues in China may be the subject of the presidential address. Although Chinese human rights violations may not be in the headlines while the simulation is being conducted, you should assume that China did commit the violations specified in the short scenario provided later in this book. Descriptions of other incidents in which China has violated its citizens' human rights will serve as a guide to research this event.

This chapter describes the roles in the simulation, the two issues that will be featured, and the three parts of the simulation and the responsibilities of each role in them. It is important that this chapter be read after you have read Chapter 1, because many of the processes discussed in this chapter will be difficult to decipher without having completed the background reading.

The Role Play

To play your role as a member of the press or as a member of the presidential communications operation effectively, you will need to research two broad areas. First, you must seek to understand the motivations, priorities, and goals of the real-life people whose roles you will assume. Second, you must understand the two policy issues under discussion, as well as the current events that will provide the context for the simulation. Depending on the preference of the simulation leader, you will delve into one or both of the policy issues described briefly in this chapter and in more detail in Part II.

Researching Your Role

As noted in Chapter 1, members of the press and those who serve on the president's staff are guided by different goals and priorities in carrying out their responsibilities. Members of the press are focused on getting the story and seeking the truth to fulfill their duty of keeping the American public in general and their readers in particular informed about the machinations and activities of the U.S. government. The president and his staff are more focused on securing positive media coverage for the administration's actions and policies. They also care about the "truth," but go to lengths to control the pace, substance, and details of the information that is released to the public.

To help you in preparing for your role, you should reread Chapter 1 carefully, paying particular attention to the roles and responsibilities of the person you will play. If you are playing a member of the White House staff, you may wish to read more broadly about the men and women who held your position in previous presidential administrations (see the list of press secretaries and communications directors in Table 1 in Chapter 1). If you are playing a member of the White House press corps, you may wish to read more about some of the more prominent correspondents who have covered the White House. Participants in the simulation who will play members of the press should also have some basic understanding of the news organizations for which they work as well as the audience for whom they produce stories. For example, if you are a reporter writing for the *Chicago Tribune,* a basic understanding of the Chicago readers, their particular concerns and cares, will help you to more effectively frame your news stories to their liking.

You also must learn about the substantive issues discussed in the three stages of the simulation and described in this chapter and in Part II. By understanding the ins and outs of these issues (or only one, if specified by your simulation leader), you can better prepare thoughtful, cogent questions (for members of the press) or answers (for presidential staff) in each stage of the simulation.

Journalists and presidential press staff also need to keep up-to-date with current events. Depending on your leader's preferences, you may be asked to limit your research of current events to a specific time period, such as the one or two weeks preceding the simulation. In reading about current events, you should keep in mind your own role in the simulation. If you work for the president, read these stories with an eye toward anticipating the types of questions reporters are likely to ask and how you might answer them. As a reporter, you might want to pinpoint any confusion or unanswered questions that arise within a story so that you can draft questions asking for clarification from the president or the press secretary if the opportunity arises. Most news organizations maintain their own Web sites, so accessing news stories on a daily basis should not be a problem.

Finally, any reporter covering the president and any staff member working for the president needs to be fully aware of the policy priorities, preferences, and positions of the president. They should pay especially close attention to any presidential positions or statements issued on particular news items. The White House maintains a Web site with a section devoted specifically to transmitting recent presidential statements, radio addresses, and other remarks (see www.whitehouse.gov/news) as does C-SPAN (www.c-span.org/executive/briefings.asp). For previous presidential activities and statements, consult the *Public Papers of the Presidents of the United States,* available online through GPO Access (www.access.gpo.gov/nara/pub-paps/srchpaps.html) and in print format through the Office of the Federal Register and the National Archives and Records Administration. Campaign promises also are fair game throughout the simulation. To learn more about the issues discussed and promises made during presidential campaigns, consult C-SPAN's wealth of video segments from the campaign trail (www.c-span.org/rwh), Congressional Quarterly's *CQ Weekly,* and other news magazines, newspapers, and Web sites. (Other sources are listed in the "For Further Information" section at the end of this chapter.)

Although it is impossible for any simulation to mirror reality perfectly, the better you play your role, the more smoothly and realistically the simulation will run. Keep in mind, however, that no one expects you to know as much as the person you are playing. Like in real life, there are likely to be questions you cannot answer. The press secretary, for example, will often say, "I will have to get back to you on that answer," or "The administration has no position on this issue at the moment." If you are playing the press secretary or another administration official, it is more important to tell members of the press that you do not know than to lie or give them the wrong information.

General Responsibilities of All Participants

- Learn about the role or actual person you will play.
- Familiarize yourself with the policy issues under consideration.
- Keep up-to-date with current events.
- Research the background and policy positions of the current administration.

In the simulation you will either choose or be assigned one of six different roles that vary in difficulty and visibility. If possible, you should choose a role that fits your own strengths and weaknesses. For example, if you do not like public speaking, you should not assume the role of the press secretary. This section briefly describes the roles of each player. The specific responsibilities and suggested assignments for each player in each part of the simulation are described later in this chapter.

President of the United States. If you are playing the president of the United States, you will have a visible role in the simulation. You will be responsible for communicating your vision and policy preferences to your staff members, allowing them to draw from your leadership. Throughout the simulation, as president you will collaborate with your communications team to craft the White House's strategy and message. Along the way, you will remind your communications team of your campaign promises on particular issues, because straying too far from those promises could cost you your reelection. Your main responsibilities during the simulation include preparing and delivering the Rose Garden address; communicating steadily with your staff (especially the press secretary and communications director) about strategy, message, and policy stances; and providing leadership over the entire White House press operation.

Because the simulation unfolds over three periods of time, you, as the president, in conjunction with your staff, must have a clear idea of what you are trying to accomplish in each stage. In general, you are trying to convey your message and priorities to the American public, to let them see how you have assumed leadership on this particular issue, and how you are working on their behalf to solve any problems that concern them. You always want to

be perceived favorably, but you need to work behind the scenes with your staff to carefully plan media appearances and manage media relations to increase the probability that you will receive positive coverage.

Director of Communications. The director of communications, who heads the White House communications team, reports directly to the president. As the communications director, you will be responsible for implementing a long-term communications strategy aimed at securing public policy victories and for ensuring that the administration's daily strategy for communicating with voters and managing the media fits into that strategy. As noted in Chapter 1, the White House communications office is, above all, seeking to achieve positive media coverage and deflect negative coverage of the president. Behind the scenes—that is, not in front of the cameras—you, as the communications director, are instrumental in crafting the words used by the press secretary and the president in all public appearances.

Press Secretary. As the press secretary and therefore the head of the White House Press Office, you will be the voice of the administration and the most public of all figures in the White House with the exception of the president. You will play this public role every weekday morning and afternoon at the White House gaggle and press briefing, at which you will carry out your role as liaison between the president and the press. In this role, you are a key player in formulating the language used by the White House in delivering its message to the press and the citizens.

Deputy Press Secretaries. There are two deputy press secretaries who play supporting roles for the press secretary. Each deputy press secretary will be involved in all communications meetings and will assist the press secretary in various ways. Of the two deputies in this simulation, one will be an expert on foreign policy and the other is an expert on domestic legislative issues. Each will help the press secretary answer questions in their respective areas. Both are responsible as well for transcribing the president's remarks in the Rose Garden address and the press secretary's comments and reporters' questions during the morning gaggle and afternoon press briefing and making these transcripts available to all those participating in the simulation.

Print Journalists. Print journalists representing a variety of major newspapers cover the White House on a daily basis (see box "News Organizations Represented in the White House Press Pool" in Chapter 1). As noted in Chapter 1, some newspapers have two White House correspondents, one who writes the daily story and one who is responsible for the feature story. Print journalists in the simulation will attend all three events that make up the simulation, asking questions of the president and press secretary whenever the opportunity arises. Then based on their observations and research, each will write a story—a news story or a feature—that will appear on the front page of their papers. (The topic will be assigned by the simulation leader.)

Broadcast Journalists. Broadcast journalists will film or audio-tape the events of the day, so they can prepare a news segment for the hourly news updates on cable and radio news programs or the networks' evening news programs. They also will attend all of the simulation events and film those they are allowed to film or record (as specified by the press secretary). Each has full discretion to decide which issues are covered on the news and the way in which the administration is portrayed.

Researching the Issues

The three parts of the simulation, described in more detail in the next section, will rely largely on consideration of one or both of two policy issues. The first is the faith-based and community initiatives program that was a central plank of Republican George W. Bush's platform in the 2000 presidential election. The program provides religious organizations with greater access to federal money that can be used to deliver social services to their communities. These programs can range from tutoring, to feeding the hungry, to mentoring and job training. The second issue is U.S.-China relations, specifically how China's human rights violations are affecting its bid to join the World Trade Organization.

For the faith-based and community initiatives program, the simulation will use the following scenario. The president is about to deliver this program to Congress, and Republican members of the House and Senate will introduce faith-based and community initiatives legislation this week (see Part II for the executive order establishing the White House Office of Faith-Based and Community Initiatives). The bill to be introduced in the House of Representatives, H.R. 7, the Community Solutions Act of 2001, increases the number of federal programs under which churches and religious groups can receive funding (see Part II for a copy of the House resolution). More specifically, the bill expands provisions of the 1996 Welfare Reform Act which allows churches and other religious organizations to compete for grants to deliver social services. The bill also requests increased levels of funding for faith-based and community initiatives programs and therefore would dramatically expand the number of faith-based programs able to receive funding.

If you are playing a member of the White House communications team, you will have to prepare for the president's Rose Garden speech where he or she will announce a new initiative to jump-start his or her faith-based program (more details on the scenario are provided in Part II). The president will provide the press with a summary of the bill's components and convey his or her passion for the legislation. In addition, the president and his or her team will have to be prepared to field a battery of questions from the press about the controversies surrounding this program—that is, about its constitutionality, fairness, and merit.

As for the second issue, U.S.-China relations, China is poised to become a member of the World Trade Organization (WTO), a membership the country has sought for some years. On October 10, 2000, President Bill Clinton signed into law H.R. 4444, a bill that allows the president to extend permanent normal trade relations to China. Passage of this bill was considered a precursor to China's entry into the WTO, because it signaled to the rest of the world that the Chinese had made sufficient advances in protecting human rights and had opened up their markets. The law also establishes an executive branch–congressional commission to review China's record on human rights, labor issues, and environmental issues.[1] Composed of U.S. senators, representatives, and executive branch officials chosen by the president, this commission is expected to report annually to Congress and the president about its findings.[2]

For the simulation, assume that the Senate Foreign Relations Committee has uncovered new evidence of human rights violations in China. In particular, it has received reports from reputable sources indicating that China's practice of harvesting organs from prisoners greatly increased in the past year. The CBS program *60 Minutes* also recently aired a special report on the issue, bringing it into the public spotlight.

In 2000, the chairman of the Senate Foreign Relations Committee, Republican Senator Jesse Helms of North Carolina, voted against normalizing trade relations with China and made impassioned speeches in opposition to H.R. 4444 on the Senate floor. In addition, he proposed an amendment that required China to ratify the International Covenant on Civil and Political Rights (ICCPR, available online at www.unhchr.ch/html/menu3/b/a_ccpr.htm) and required the president to certify to Congress that China had made improvements in its human rights practices before granting normalized trade relations.[3] The amendment proposed by Helms did not pass. China has now signed the ICCPR but still has not ratified it. In light of the new human rights violations, assume that Senator Helms has reintroduced his legislation (Amendment

No. 4125, reproduced in Part II) with the hope of imposing trade sanctions on the Chinese until there is evidence of improvements in human rights.

Now the president is preparing to meet with the press and invited guests in the Rose Garden to discuss and respond to the recently uncovered human rights violations. Members of the White House communications team should begin to prepare for the president's speech and to anticipate the types of questions that will be asked by members of the press. Members of the press should familiarize themselves with the issues at hand and prepare thoughtful questions to ask the president and his communications team.

Research of the issues, aided by the documents in Part II, will help you to prepare thoughtful, cogent questions (for members of the press) or answers (for presidential staff) in each stage of the simulation. The simulation leader may ask you to write a paper to demonstrate your knowledge of the policy issues under discussion. If not, it is recommended that you familiarize yourself with the details, history, and various arguments in favor of and opposed to the status quo. As noted, a variety of Web sites and suggestions for further reading appear at the end of this chapter. Today, information is power, so the more well versed you are in the nuances of the policy issues, the better prepared you will be to ask or anticipate tough questions and follow-ups.

The Three Primary Simulation Exercises: The Morning Gaggle, the Presidential Rose Garden Address, and the Afternoon Briefing

In the simulation your class or group will enact three phases of the daily interaction between the president's communications team and the White House press corps: the morning gaggle, in which members of the press corps are able to question the press secretary about procedural and substantive issues that might arise throughout the day; the president's Rose Garden address where the president will speak to the press corps and other invited guests about a particular issue and take questions if appropriate; and the afternoon briefing in which the press secretary takes questions from the press corps, typically focusing on events that occurred or will occur later that day.

Depending on the preference of the simulation leader and the group size, the group may focus on one or both of the issues described more fully in the documents in Part II of this book. Also depending on the preference of the simulation leader, the group may conduct one, two, or all three parts of the simulation. It is recommended that at least one issue be carried through all three events as opposed to using one issue for one part and the other issue for another part. Either the simulation group could remain intact and deal with one or both issues, or the group could be divided in two, with two presidents, two press secretaries, and two press corps, each group dealing with a single issue. Either way, the responsibilities of the players remain the same.

In the first phase, the gaggle, the White House press corps meets with the press secretary in his or her office to discuss the day's events and ask any questions about logistics or the facts needed for a story. This event is short and gives the press a preview of what to expect throughout the day.

In the second phase, the president gives a speech in the Rose Garden to address one of the two issues. The text and substance of the speech is left up to the president and his or her communications team. The Rose Garden address serves as an opportunity for the president and the White House team to present their best face to the American public and offers the press the opportunity to question the president if he or she agrees to take questions.

The third phase is the afternoon briefing where the press has the best opportunity to ask in-depth questions of the press secretary about the day's events or any other issues of interest to the press.

All three phases are described more fully in the sections that follow.

The Morning Gaggle

Prior to the gaggle, the White House communications team will meet with the president to determine the White House strategy and message for that day. The line-of-the-day mechanism described in Chapter 1 is useful for ensuring that the president's staff and members of the administration speak in the same terms when dealing with members of the press. Without a line-of-the-day, the communications team runs the risk of working at odds with one another or, worse yet, allowing the press to control the agenda.

The director of communications, the press secretary, and the president also will decide what responses will be used by the press secretary both in the gaggle and in the afternoon briefing and by the president in the Rose Garden address and what information will be communicated to or withheld from the press. More specifically, they will decide which questions the president and the press secretary will or will not answer and the responses they will use to answer or avoid the question.

As described in more detail in Chapter 1, the gaggle, which is held most mornings, is an opportunity for the press to learn the president's schedule early in the day and to discuss upcoming events with the press secretary. The gaggle serves as a warm-up for the day's activities to follow, and the communications staff must be certain to keep in touch with one another to ensure all are sharing relevant information and strategizing accordingly (see box "Sample Transcript, White House Press Gaggle" in Chapter 1).

Participants will simulate the gaggle by playing the roles of the press secretary, deputy press secretaries, and the White House press corps. The members of the press will position themselves outside of the press secretary's office and wait for an invitation to enter. The press secretary will then provide the press with the president's daily schedule and take questions. When necessary, the press secretary will defer to a deputy press secretary who is an expert in either foreign policy or a domestic legislative topic under discussion. The gaggle usually lasts for about twenty minutes, but the simulation leader may allow the process to continue longer.

During the gaggle, the press is likely to focus on the speech that will be given by the president later that day in the Rose Garden and the events surrounding the topic of the speech. It is up to the press secretary and the director of communications to decide whether they want to distribute an advance copy of the president's speech to the press. The press secretary can choose to do so before, during, or after the gaggle; it is strictly up to the communications team. For example, Bill Clinton's communications team rarely distributed advance copies of speeches, because Clinton made changes in them up to the last moment. President Ronald Reagan's team almost always provided the press with advance copies, because the president did not waver from his written text.[4]

If you are a member of the White House press corps, you should use the gaggle as a time to ask procedural questions about the daily activities of the president and the White House staff and substantive questions that might help you to write a better story. For example, as a member of the press corps you might want to know whether a last-minute event that was not on the schedule is open to the entire press corps or whether it is restricted to members of the press pool. Or you might want to know whether the president will take questions from workers attending a speech scheduled, perhaps, at an automobile manufacturing plant later that afternoon.

In terms of substantive questions, you may want to know the details of some provisions of the president's budget or of a legislative proposal recently sent to Capitol Hill. It is your job as a member of the press to try and get

as much information from the press secretary as possible. At times, the secretary may resist, but you should not immediately back down. Getting an answer to your question may sometimes entail asking your question more than once, or asking it in a variety of different ways while enduring the press secretary's impatience.

As a member of the press, you will draft questions ahead of time and diligently attempt to get those questions answered at some point during the day, either by the president or the press secretary. Because many of the questions you prepare may be asked by another reporter, you should have a long list of ones important to the story you are trying to write. You should come to the gaggle prepared to take notes or, if you prefer, to use a tape recorder to capture the press secretary's words.

If you are playing the role of press secretary, the president's spokesperson in relations with the press, you may not want to provide as much information as the press is seeking. Although the press may push you to answer certain questions, you should have already discussed with your communications director and the president what information you will give the press and what you will withhold. You must think of a tactful way to tell the press that you will not give them what they want. Meanwhile, keep in mind that the press secretary and the press go through these exercises every day, and the atmosphere is generally informal and friendly. Things can become tense at times, but, overall, the press and the press secretary work toward preserving an amicable relationship.

The participants in the gaggle have the following responsibilities:

• *The President.* Although you, as president, have no visible role in this part of the simulation, you will be involved behind the scenes. Prior to the gaggle, you will meet with your communications team—the communications director, the press secretary, and any deputy press secretaries—to formulate strategy for the entire simulation. This strategy includes deciding on a line-of-the-day, anticipating questions likely to be asked by the press and fashioning appropriate responses, deciding which issues or questions will not be commented on or answered, and thinking about the big picture.

• *The Director of Communications.* Like the president, you, as director of communications, will have no visible role in this part of the simulation, but you will meet with the rest of the communications team prior to the gaggle and direct that strategy meeting. This meeting involves deciding what the president will say in the Rose Garden address and what language the press secretary will use to describe what the president has said. You are also charged with the responsi-

SUMMARY OF GAGGLE RESPONSIBILITIES

President

- Meet with the press secretary and the communications director prior to the simulation session to strategize and decide on the line-of-the-day.
- Discuss the upcoming Rose Garden address and make sure the entire communications staff is on message.

Press Secretary

- Start gaggle by inviting reporters into office.
- Make opening statement, if any, to begin gaggle discussion.
- Call on reporters and be prepared to answer at least a few of their questions.
- Bring gaggle to a close and usher reporters out of office.
- Meet with the president and communications director before and after the gaggle to compare notes and strategize.

Deputy Press Secretaries

- Provide members of the White House press corps with a copy of president's schedule (via e-mail or an actual handout).
- Prior to the gaggle, research your area of expertise.
- Help brief the press secretary prior to the gaggle on your area of expertise, anticipating any questions that the press secretary is likely to receive.
- Attend the gaggle and respond to any inquiries or questions from the press secretary.
- After the gaggle, transcribe the remarks and questions and distribute them to the rest of the simulation participants.

Communications Director

- Draft the line-of-the day (with the help of the press secretary and the president).
- Remind the press secretary of the line-of-the-day before he or she begins the gaggle.
- Draw up the president's schedule for the day (in conjunction with deputy press secretaries and president).
- Decide which events will be open to all of the press and which will be off-limits or open only to the press pool.
- Establish the parameters for press involvement in the scheduled presidential activities and appearances (where press will be stationed and when it will be able to pose questions).
- Meet with the president and press secretary before and after the gaggle to compare notes, strategize, and prepare for future activities (especially the upcoming Rose Garden address).

Journalists (both print and broadcast)

- Draft questions to ask the press secretary (these should be typed up and ready to hand in).
- Take notes on the gaggle proceedings.

bility for developing the line-of-the-day and determining the president's schedule for the day.

Although scheduling may take weeks or even months in real life, this exercise can be completed much more quickly in the simulation. In drawing up the president's schedule, you must think about what events will likely produce positive coverage and how to schedule appearances that will satisfy the various constituencies that would like the ear and attention of the president. Along with the press secretary, you must also determine which events on the president's schedule are open to members of the press and provide any instructions the press may need in order to cover the event.

• *The Press Secretary.* As the press secretary, you will run the gaggle and so must prepare extensively for it. After the early morning meeting with the communications team, you must be prepared to answer questions on a wide range of topics from the press. You also must decide whether to provide the press with any official statements at the start of the gaggle. You will go through the schedule with the press and answer any detailed questions about the president's day such as which events are open to all members of the press and which are restricted to the daily press pool, when cameras will be allowed, and any other logistical matters that may arise.

• *Deputy Press Secretaries.* Two deputies will attend the gaggle and answer any questions the press secretary sends their way. One deputy will be an expert on foreign policy and the other on domestic legislative affairs. As a deputy press secretary, it is your job to research the issue area on which the president will speak later in the day in order to assist the press secretary during the gaggle and later during the briefing. In fact, you should be prepared to answer a wide variety of questions, and you should try to anticipate reporters' queries. To do so, you will have to keep yourself apprised of current events and recent presidential activities and statements in your particular policy area.

• *Print Journalists.* Participants can choose which newspaper they wish to represent (see box "News Organizations Represented in the White House Press Pool" in Chapter 1 for a list of newspapers). Some members of the press corps will be writing daily stories; others will write feature stories. If you are writing a daily story, your questions will focus more on the day's events. If you are asked to write a feature story, your questions will focus on a particular issue area. All reporters should come to the gaggle armed with questions and follow-up questions for the press secretary.

• *Broadcast Journalists.* Cameras are not permitted in the gaggle, but as a member of the television networks or radio organizations you may want to attend the gaggle to get an idea of what the nightly news story might be. Remember, however, that you can only take notes and ask questions like any other reporter.

The Presidential Rose Garden Address

In the second part of the simulation, the president delivers an address in the Rose Garden on one of the two topics described in this chapter and in Part II (see box "Sample Presidential Rose Garden Address). The leader of the simulation will choose the topic. The entire press corps will attend the speech and will be seated in front of the president who will stand at a podium bearing the presidential seal. If the president and the president's communications team elect to do so, the president can ask an adviser or other official to join him or her after the speech in responding to any especially complex questions from the press. Or the president may invite a foreign leader or other individual to be on hand to support the president's cause.

During this part of the simulation, the president can refuse to answer the press's questions or can answer them selectively depending on the strategy adopted. For example, the president may refuse to answer any questions of a personal nature at a Rose Garden address. In posing questions, members of the press should aggressively push the president to provide as much information as possible and be aggressive when asking questions.

Press conferences typically last approximately twenty minutes. After the press conference, the press and president leave the Rose Garden and continue with their daily events.

The participants in the Rose Garden event have the following responsibilities:

• *The President.* As the president, you will deliver the Rose Garden address and field questions from the press. If you decide to have a joint press conference with a foreign leader or other individual, you will introduce that person as well. In this phase of the simulation, your most important responsibility as president is to prepare your speech. Presidents typically employ speechwriters to assist them in carrying out their vast public speaking responsibilities. Some presidents are more intimately engaged in the speechwriting process than others. For example, Clinton was notorious for writing and rewriting his own speeches, often adding the finishing touches moments before he was scheduled to speak. Others, like Reagan, left the job almost entirely to their staff.[5] For the simulation, you, as president, will write your own speech, but you may look to your staff members for assistance. Then, you should rehearse delivery of the address. Because you will not have the benefit of TelePrompTers, you will have to practice your prepared remarks to ensure you appear polished and fluent. The many news organizations that will be taping the address for their nightly news broadcasts will probably air whatever appears most newsworthy, whether it depicts you, as president, in a positive or negative light. To receive positive coverage, you need to appear presidential and should not stumble awkwardly through your remarks.

• *The Director of Communications.* As the director of communications, you have no visible role in this part of the simulation, but you will help to prepare the president for the Rose Garden address, giving advice on word choice, helping to prepare and revise the speech itself, and ensuring that at least a couple of worthy sound bites are inserted for the benefit of the news organizations. In addition, you should work behind the scenes in an attempt to place a positive editorial about the issue in a newspaper or news magazine.

• *The Press Secretary.* As the press secretary, you will attend the address but have no visible role in this part of the simulation. You should work behind the scenes, however, to help the president prepare the speech, to listen to a prac-

SAMPLE PRESIDENTIAL ROSE GARDEN ADDRESS

Remarks Following a Cabinet Meeting on the Administration's Agenda
by President George W. Bush

August 3, 2001

Good afternoon. The Vice President and I are pleased to welcome the Cabinet to the Rose Garden. Together with Congress, we are proving that a new tone, a clear agenda, and active leadership can bring significant progress to the Nation's Capital. We are ending deadlock and drift and making our system work on behalf of the American people. Six months ago I chose a distinguished Cabinet, took a solemn oath, and promised to fight for the things close to my heart. My administration pledged to bring stability and high standards to Washington and to lead for the sake of all Americans.

Six months later I'm proud of my Cabinet and the White House staff, who have worked with such energy and have brought integrity to their jobs. I'm grateful for the good will shown by Congress, and I am pleased with the progress we have made together, progress that touches every American family.

We acted quickly to pass the first major tax cut in a generation to help families in an economic slowdown and to help rebuild the momentum of our economy.

Both Houses of Congress have passed major education reform legislation, which will bring a new passion for excellence to America's public schools. We have broken 6 years of gridlock in the task of protecting patients from arbitrary medical decisions made by bureaucrats. The House has passed a bill to promote the work of mentoring groups, homeless shelters, and drug treatment facilities. And I have had positive discussions with leaders in the United States Senate on this matter.

The House has also passed an energy plan that addresses current needs. We have put our foreign policy on sound footing. We are strengthening our relationships with our allies and moving to build a world that trades more freely.

We have taken the first steps toward revitalizing and transforming our military so it can meet the threats and challenges of the future. Today the Senate joined with the House to provide our farmers with $5.5 billion of emergency help. We passed a budget resolution that, for the first time in recent memory, has been respected, not ignored. And we are on our way to the second largest surplus in history, as well as paying down a significant amount of U.S. debt.

On this path, we are headed for a year of strong, meaningful legislative achievements. And I want to express my thanks for every legislator who made tough decisions, every legislator who chose long-term progress over short-term political gain.

There's much more to do. In September the second stage of our work begins, and I will be guided by a few goals. First, we must finish the work we have begun. On the topics of education and the disadvantaged, our Nation has needs that will not wait. Americans, come September, will be watching. They want us to be principled, not partisan. They want us to look for agreement instead of looking for fights and arguments. Americans know obstructionism when they see it, and when necessary, I will point it out.

Second, the Congress must live within the generous limits of our budget. Irresponsible spending is a threat to our economy and a threat to the essential functions of our Government. I will protect Medicare, Social Security, and our Armed Forces. And I will protect the American taxpayers. The Congress, through its budget resolution, has given its word on spending. So far, Congress has kept its word, and it must continue to do so.

Third, within a limited budget we must have an active, compassionate Government. Beginning in September, I'll be proposing creative ways to tackle some of the toughest problems in our society. We must take the side of parents trying to raise responsible, motivated, and moral children. We must help disadvantaged Americans find opportunity and ownership and the tools to succeed in our free economy. We must show that our welcoming society values the ideals and contributions of immigrants. We must challenge Americans to be citizens, not spectators, in the renewal of their neighborhoods and their cities.

In a few days, I'm headed home to the heartland to listen to the American people and to talk about the values that unite and sustain our country. Members of Congress are going home, as well. When we all come back in September, so many accomplishments are within our reach, and I look forward to the work ahead.

Thank you all very much.

Source: National Archives and Records Administration, "Weekly Compilation of Presidential Documents," <www.access.gpo. gov/nara/nara003.html>. Accessed August 6 2001.

SUMMARY OF ROSE GARDEN ADDRESS RESPONSIBILITIES

President

- Prepare your Rose Garden address.
- Deliver your prepared remarks to the audience.
- Prepare to answer questions from the press.
- Practice speech!

Press Secretary

- Communicate with the president and communications director to ensure that the substance of the press release co-incides with the president's actual planned remarks.
- Coach the president prior to the address, sitting through a dry run of the speech. Make sure that the president's prepared comments are appropriate and likely to generate positive media coverage (or at least be prepared for whatever negative coverage may ensue).

Deputy Press Secretaries

- Write and distribute a press release summarizing the president's speech to members of the White House press corps.
- Tape-record the Rose Garden address.
- After the address, transcribe the president's remarks and distribute them to rest of the participants in the simulation.

Communications Director

- Communicate with the president and deputy press secretary to ensure that the substance of the press release co-incides with the president's actual planned remarks.
- Prepare a "ghost-written" editorial praising the president's Rose Garden address.

Print Journalists

- Prepare questions (typed and ready to be handed in) to ask the president.

Broadcast Journalists

- Film (or tape-record) the Rose Garden address.
- Ensure equipment works and is unobtrusive.

---

tice run of the speech, and to offer the president advice on performance.

• *Deputy Press Secretaries.* Before arriving at the Rose Garden address, you will prepare a one-page press release that summarizes the president's forthcoming comments. As a deputy press secretary, you will attend and tape-record the Rose Garden address so you can later transcribe the president's exact remarks and distribute the text of the address to your colleagues in the White House and to reporters.

• *Print Journalists.* As a member of the White House press corps, you will come to the Rose Garden prepared to ask the president questions. If the president is appearing with another official or foreign dignitary, you may wish to ask the official or

dignitary questions as well. As noted earlier, the kinds of questions you ask will depend on the type of story you are writing. These responsibilities are virtually the same as those identified for the gaggle, but the questions must be posed with all the respect and decorum normally accorded the president. For example, you should always use the title "Mr. President" when asking questions or otherwise speaking to the president.

• *Broadcast Journalists.* As a broadcast journalist, you will film (or tape-record) the address in order to create a television or radio spot for the evening news. To prepare for the presidential address, make sure that your equipment is in proper working order and that you are sufficiently familiar with the equipment in order to operate it without incident.

The Afternoon Briefing

In the third part of the exercise, participants simulate the afternoon briefing, the correspondents' opportunity to question the press secretary in front of the cameras. In the White House briefing room the press secretary will stand at a podium in the front of the room, facing the press who are seated. The press deputies present at the briefing will assist the press secretary when necessary. The members of the press will ask questions that span several topics, although, again, they are likely to focus on the speech given by the president earlier in the day. The press focuses on the president's daily activities as well as any other news that is anticipated that week.

The briefing officially begins when the press secretary enters the briefing room. The press secretary typically begins the briefing with an announcement or statement, but he or she is not required to make an official statement. The press secretary then begins to take questions from the press.

Members of the press must be aggressive to get their questions answered. For example, they may have to talk over other members of the corps, speak loudly, raise their hands, and even call out the press secretary's name. It is completely at the discretion of the press secretary whether to answer questions on certain topics, whom he or she allows to ask questions, and how long the briefing will last.

After about thirty minutes, the press secretary indicates that only a few more questions will be taken and quickly draws the briefing to a close. The secretary then exits through the door and goes up the stairs, passing the upper press office and going into the West Wing.

The participants in the afternoon press briefing have the following responsibilities:

• *The President.* As president, you have no visible role in this part of the simulation, but you should work behind the scenes to confer with the press secretary and communications director to revisit the line-of-the-day and discuss any events that have arisen since the Rose Garden address or the morning gaggle. Although the time horizon for discussion and planning in real life is more compressed than that devoted to the classroom simulation, the need to plan and coordinate communications remains the same. If separate days are devoted to each of the three parts of the simulation, the leader may require some outside consultations among the president, press secretary, and communications director prior to enactment of each part. Some of these discussions may revolve around reiterating or revising the previously devised line-of-the-day, deciding how to address (or whether to address) any happenings that have arisen since

the Rose Garden address (or gaggle), and anticipating reporters' queries.

• *The Director of Communications.* Like the president, you have no visible role in this part of the simulation, but you should work behind the scenes with the president and the press secretary to develop the White House's message and line-of-the-day and develop creative ways for securing positive media coverage of the day's events.

• *The Press Secretary.* Because you, as the press secretary, will be running the briefing in front of the television cameras, this is your most important appearance. You may decide to open the briefing with a statement or may simply begin the proceedings by inviting questions. Whatever the case, in conducting the briefing you will acknowledge reporters so they can ask questions and then you will decide whether or not to answer them. After responding to questions from the press—but not necessarily to all of them—you will end the briefing whenever you see fit. A situation in which reporters keep hurling the same questions after you have answered them as completely as you deem prudent may be a good reason to stop answering questions altogether. Yet you should also bear in mind your role as the liaison between the press and the president. In other words, as the intermediary between the two groups, you, as the press secretary, must attempt to preserve good working relationships with both the president and the press. Prematurely halting the afternoon briefing may sour relations with the press, at least if done on a regular basis.

• *Deputy Press Secretaries.* As a deputy, you will attend the briefing with the press secretary and answer any questions delegated to you by the secretary. As such, you should communicate with the press secretary ahead of time to determine what types of questions you might be called on to answer. You also should be aware of the line-of-the-day and any other communications strategies devised by the rest of your colleagues on the communications staff (communications director, press secretary, president, etc). Finally, it is your responsibility to tape-record and then transcribe the briefing and distribute it to the rest of the White House staff and reporters.

• *Print Journalists.* As a member of the press corps, you will come to the briefing prepared to ask questions about what the president said earlier in the day during the Rose Garden address. You will also ask questions about other issues of importance to the administration. Meanwhile, you take notes on the briefing and leave to write your story when the briefing is over. Because the press receives the transcript of the briefing prepared by the deputy press secretaries (see box "Sample Transcript, White House Daily

---

SUMMARY OF AFTERNOON BRIEFING RESPONSIBILITIES

President

- Meet with the press secretary and communications director prior to the simulation to communicate about any new events that have arisen.
- Decide how to respond to any new events.

Press Secretary

- Begin the afternoon briefing.
- Make an opening statement, if any.
- Call on reporters and be prepared to answer their questions.
- Bring afternoon briefing to a close.
- Meet with the president and communications director before and after the briefing to compare notes and strategize.

Deputy Press Secretaries

- Communicate with the press secretary prior to the briefing about the types of questions you will be expected to answer.
- Meet with the communications staff to ensure you are familiar with the line-of-the-day and any other planned strategy.
- Record briefing (for transcribing purposes).
- Later, transcribe briefing and distribute it to the rest of the participants in the simulation.

Communications Director

- Work behind the scenes with the communications team to decide on the line-of-the-day.
- Assist the press secretary in crafting answers to questions he or she is likely to receive.

Print Journalists

- Prepare questions to ask of the press secretary and any other administration officials participating in the briefing (type up and be prepared to hand in).
- Tape-record or take notes on the proceedings.
- Ask follow-up questions of the press secretary, when possible.

Broadcast Journalists

- Bring all necessary equipment to the simulation session (all you will need to capture footage to incorporate into your story).
- Film (or tape-record) the briefing and, if appropriate, include this footage in the evening news report.

Briefing" in Chapter 1), you do not need to record the event, although most reporters do take notes.

• *Broadcast Journalists.* In your role as a broadcast journalist, you will film or tape-record the briefing and use it to create a segment for your upcoming news broadcast. After the briefing concludes, you will begin the process of editing and packaging the comments uttered by the press secretary. Because so many topics are usually covered during the briefing, you will have to sift through all the commentary to find the nuggets most relevant for your own story.

Notes

1. Lori Nitschke, "After the China Bill: Fresh Start for the Trade Expansion Debate," *CQ Weekly,* September 23, 2000, 2223 (article reproduced in Part II).
2. Human Rights Watch, "China: Bush Should Use Qian Visit to Press for Rights Progress," March 20, 2000 <www.hrw.org/press/2001/03/qianmeeting.htm>, accessed March 31, 2001.
3. Chuck McCutcheon and Lori Nitschke, "China Trade Bill Remains Intact as Senate Rejects Arms Sanctions," *CQ Weekly,* September 16, 2000, 2152 (reproduced in Part II).

4. Mark Hertsgaard, *On Bended Knee: The Press and the Reagan Presidency* (New York: Schocken Books, 1989).
5. Ibid.

Suggested Exercises and Assignments

1. Write a policy position paper on one of the two issues described in Chapter 2 and in more detail in Part II. In particular, focus on the following questions: When did the issue climb onto the national agenda? What is the history of this policy issue? What are the various arguments and controversies surrounding the issue? Which political players are lined up on each side of the policy debate? What public pronouncements, if any, has the president made on this issue?

2. Write a paper identifying and detailing the current president's policy position on one of the two issues described in Chapter 2 and Part II. Drawing on official presidential pronouncements, campaign promises, State of the Union addresses, and budget messages address the following questions: What stance has the president taken on this issue? Has his policy position remained consistent over time? What is the reasoning behind his policy position? Also, assess the president's perspectives with an eye toward his reelection prospects. What is he trying to accomplish in office? Who voted for him? Who did NOT vote for him but might be willing to in the next election? What can the president do to appeal to these voters?

3. Compare and contrast political news stories related to the presidency from at least two different news organizations. Do the two sources provide essentially the same information, or are there noticeable substantive differences in their coverage? If you identify differences between the two, what might explain these differences? Discuss. (You may wish to consult the online e-zine *Slate* at www.slate.com, which publishes a daily summary of news stories carried in the nation's major dailies.)

4. Compare and contrast news stories on an issue high on the current president's agenda from at least two different news organizations. What do the reporters do well in these stories? Do they provide the public with a window on the White House? Would you characterize the stories as essentially positive, negative, or neutral? Do they provide sufficient substantive information or focus primarily on process and conflict? Discuss.

5. Write a paper detailing the news organization and audience whose correspondent you are playing. Be sure to include a brief history of the news organization, the types of news coverage provided (that is, is it a daily paper, news magazine, wire service, cable network?), and the audience and clientele of the organization (those who buy your print news or advertise on your broadcast news). Look over the news coverage produced by the organization within the past year or so. From its coverage, can you determine whether the audience is more interested in local or national news? Domestic or international stories? What else can you determine about the audience? Discuss.

For Further Information

Presidential Remarks and Activities

C-SPAN. "Daily White House Briefings" <www.cspan.org/executive/briefings.asp>. Contains RealVideo archive of recent daily White House press briefings.

———. "Road to the White House" <www.c-span.org/rwh>. Contains a weekly look at the candidates and issues shaping the presidential election.

National Archives and Records Administration <www.nara.gov/research/all/presmats.html>. Presidential materials, including records and historical materials.

———. "Public Papers of the Presidents of the United States" <www.access.gpo.gov/nara/pubpaps/srchpaps.htm>. Searchable database of public papers of U.S. presidents.

———. "Weekly Compilation of Presidential Documents" <www.access.gpo.gov/nara/nara003.html>. Includes statements, messages, and other presidential material released by the White House since 1993.

White House <www.whitehouse.gov/>. Archive of presidential remarks, radio addresses, and activities <www.whitehouse.gov/news/> and White House transcripts of press briefings <www.whitehouse.gov/news/briefings>.

Press Materials

Cable News Network (CNN) <www.cnn.com>. A continually updated news site featuring live streaming video, audio packages, and searchable archives of news features and background information.

National Press Club Online <npc.press.org/who/sources.htm>. A directory of the National Press Club's news sources, with a searchable database.

National Public Radio <www.npr.org>. Coverage of the latest developments in U.S. and world news, business and technology, health, science, and the arts.

Newspaper Association of America <www.naa.org>. Information on how marketing, public policy, diversity, industry development, newspaper operations, and readership collectively affect the newspaper industry.

Newspaper Links <www.newspaperlinks.com/home. cfm>. A comprehensive gateway to newspaper Web sites around the world.

Online Newspapers <www.onlinenewspapers.com>. A searchable database of worldwide newspapers.

U.S. Newswire <www.usnewswire.com>. News coverage of all three branches of government.

Faith-Based and Community Initiatives

Americans United for Separation of Church and State <www.au.org>. Information on supporting and understanding the notion of separation of church and state.

Center for Public Justice <www.cpjustice.org/ charitablechoice>. Information on the White House faith-based and charitable choice programs.

Department of Health and Human Services <www. faithbasedcommunityinitiatives.org/DHHS_Faith_Based. htm>. Information on faith-based programs.

Department of Housing and Urban Development <www.hud.gov/offices/fbci/Index.cfm>. Information on faith-based programs.

People for the American Way <www.pfaw.org/Issues/ liberty/charitable_choice.shtml>. Provides arguments against charitable choice.

Texas Workforce Commission <www.twc.state.tx.us/ svcs/charchoice/chchoice.html>. Provides information on federal and Texas faith-based programs, including other Web links.

White House <www.faithbasedcommunityinitiatives. org>. Information on the George W. Bush administration's perspective and goals for its faith-based and community initiatives program.

U.S.-China Relations

American Foreign Policy Council <www.afpc.org>. Current information on American foreign policy in China and other parts of the world.

China Internet Information Center <www.china.org. cn/english/index.htm>. Up-to-date news on China as well as a searchable text of government position papers.

Human Rights Watch <www.hrw.org>. Background information, current events, and articles surrounding the worldwide human rights campaign.

U.S. Department of State <www.state.gov/www/ background_notes/china_0011_bgn.html>. A permanent electronic archive of information released prior to January 20, 2001, about China.

U.S. House. Committee on International Relations <www.house.gov/international_relations>. Information on the committee's policies, legislation, and membership.

U.S. Senate. Committee on Foreign Relations <www. senate.gov/~foreign/>. Information on the committee's policies, legislation, and membership.

Washington Post. "World Special Reports on China" <www.washingtonpost.com/wp-dyn/world/specials/ asia/china>. The latest news on China published by the *Washington Post.*

World Trade Organization <www.wto.org>. Provides news and information on its organization and its members.

PART II

Media Research Materials

Faith-Based and Community Initiatives: The Scenario

The issue of faith-based and community initiatives has been important to the George W. Bush administration. The program provides religious congregations with greater access to federal money to deliver social services to their communities. These programs can range from tutoring to feeding the hungry to mentoring and job training.

Signed on January 29, 2001, by President George W. Bush, Executive Order 13199 (included in the following documents) established a White House office of faith-based and community initiatives. This order was the first step in the administration's promotion and implementation of faith-based programs. Bush initially tapped John DiIulio, an academic, to run his faith-based and community initiatives organization. After drawing fire from all sides, DiIulio resigned from the position in August 2001.

The administration's next step in expanding its faith-based and community initiatives program is to appoint a new director of the organization, build support for the program, and ensure that the required legislation will be introduced in the House of Representatives and the Senate.

Previous bills, including H.R. 7 (part of which follows), have not made it through the House of Representatives, but it is possible that President Bush will attempt to have a new, and perhaps similar, bill introduced. H.R. 7 increases the number of programs under which churches and religious groups can receive funding. This bill expands the provisions in the 1996 Welfare Reform Act that allows churches and other religious organizations to compete for grants to deliver social services. The bill also requests increased levels of funding for faith-based and community initiatives programs and would dramatically expand the number of faith-based programs able to receive funding.

As a member of the White House communications team or as the president, you must prepare for a Rose Garden address in which the president will announce a new initiative to attempt to jump-start the faith-based program. It is possible that the president will announce a new appointment, a piece of legislation, or another newsworthy event related to faith-based and community initiatives. After the announcement, the president and the communications team will have to prepare to field a battery of questions from the press about the controversies surrounding this program—its constitutionality, fairness, and merit. At the morning gaggle and afternoon briefing, members of the press will ask the press secretary about the program and perhaps further challenge its merits.

PRESIDENTIAL DOCUMENTS

EXECUTIVE ORDER 13199 OF JANUARY 29, 2001

Establishment of White House Office of Faith-Based and Community Initiatives

By the authority vested in me as President of the United States by the Constitution and the laws of the United States of America, and in order to help the Federal Government coordinate a national effort to expand opportunities for faith-based and other community organizations and to strengthen their capacity to better meet social needs in America's communities, it is hereby ordered as follows:

Section 1. *Policy.* Faith-based and other community organizations are indispensable in meeting the needs of poor Americans and distressed neighborhoods. Government cannot be replaced by such organizations, but it can and should welcome them as partners. The paramount goal is compassionate results, and private and charitable community groups, including religious ones, should have the fullest opportunity permitted by law to compete on a level playing field, so long as they achieve valid public purposes, such as curbing crime, conquering addiction, strengthening families and neighborhoods, and overcoming poverty. This delivery of social services must be results oriented and should value the bedrock principles of pluralism, nondiscrimination, evenhandedness, and neutrality.

Sec. 2. *Establishment.* There is established a White House Office of Faith-Based and Community Initiatives (White House OFBCI) within the Executive Office of the President that will have lead responsibility in the executive branch to establish policies, priorities, and objectives for the Federal Government's comprehensive effort to enlist, equip, enable, empower, and expand the work of faith-based and other community organizations to the extent permitted by law.

Sec. 3. *Functions.* The principal functions of the White House OFBCI are, to the extent permitted by law: (a) to develop, lead, and coordinate the Administration's policy agenda affecting faith-based and other community programs and initiatives, expand the role of such efforts in communities, and increase their capacity through executive action, legislation, Federal and private funding, and regulatory relief;

(b) to ensure that Administration and Federal Government policy decisions and programs are consistent with the President's stated goals with respect to faith-based and other community initiatives;

(c) to help integrate the President's policy agenda affecting faith-based and other community organizations across the Federal Government;

(d) to coordinate public education activities designed to mobilize public support for faith-based and community nonprofit initiatives through volunteerism, special projects, demonstration pilots, and public-private partnerships;

(e) to encourage private charitable giving to support faith-based and community initiatives;

(f) to bring concerns, ideas, and policy options to the President for assisting, strengthening, and replicating successful faith-based and other community programs;

(g) to provide policy and legal education to State, local, and community policymakers and public officials seeking ways to empower faith-based and other community organizations and to improve the opportunities, capacity, and expertise of such groups;

(h) to develop and implement strategic initiatives under the President's agenda to strengthen the institutions of civil society and America's families and communities;

(i) to showcase and herald innovative grassroots nonprofit organizations and civic initiatives;

(j) to eliminate unnecessary legislative, regulatory, and other bureaucratic barriers that impede effective faith-based and other community efforts to solve social problems;

(k) to monitor implementation of the President's agenda affecting faith-based and other community organizations; and

(l) to ensure that the efforts of faith-based and other community organizations meet high standards of excellence and accountability.

From *Federal Register,* January 31, 2001 (Vol. 66, No. 21)

Sec. 4. *Administration.* (a) The White House OFBCI may function through established or ad hoc committees, task forces, or interagency groups.

(b) The White House OFBCI shall have a staff to be headed by the Assistant to the President for Faith-Based and Community Initiatives. The White House OFBCI shall have such staff and other assistance, to the extent permitted by law, as may be necessary to carry out the provisions of this order. The White House OFBCI operations shall begin no later than 30 days from the date of this order.

(c) The White House OFBCI shall coordinate with the liaison and point of contact designated by each executive department and agency with respect to this initiative.

(d) All executive departments and agencies (agencies) shall cooperate with the White House OFBCI and provide such information, support, and assistance to the White House OFBCI as it may request, to the extent permitted by law.

(e) The agencies' actions directed by this Executive Order shall be carried out subject to the availability of appropriations and to the extent permitted by law.

Sec. 5. *Judicial Review.* This order does not create any right or benefit, substantive or procedural, enforceable at law or equity by a party against the United States, its agencies or instrumentalities, its officers or employees, or any other person.

THE WHITE HOUSE,
January 29, 2001.

H.R. 7

Community Solutions Act of 2001
(Introduced in the House)

TITLE II—EXPANSION OF CHARITABLE CHOICE

SEC. 201. PROVISION OF ASSISTANCE UNDER GOVERNMENT PROGRAMS BY RELIGIOUS AND COMMUNITY ORGANIZATIONS.

1   *Title XXIV of the Revised Statutes is amended by inserting after*

2   *section 1990 (42 U.S.C. 1994) the following:*

3   **'SEC. 1994A. CHARITABLE CHOICE.**

4   '(a) SHORT TITLE—This section may be cited as the `Charitable

5   Choice Act of 2001'.

6   '(b) PURPOSES—The purposes of this section are—

7   '(1) to provide assistance to individuals and families in need in

8   the most effective and efficient manner;

9   '(2) to prohibit discrimination against religious organizations

10   on the basis of religion in the administration and distribution of gov-

11   ernment assistance under the government programs described in sub-

12   section (c)(4);

13   '(3) to allow religious organizations to assist in the adminis-

14   tration and distribution of such assistance without impairing the reli-

15   gious character of such organizations; and

16   '(4) to protect the religious freedom of individuals and families

17   in need who are eligible for government assistance, including expand-

18   ing the possibility of choosing to receive services from a religious or-

19   ganization providing such assistance.

20   '(c) RELIGIOUS ORGANIZATIONS INCLUDED AS NON-

21   GOVERNMENTAL PROVIDERS—

22   '(1) IN GENERAL—

23   '(A) INCLUSION—For any program described in paragraph

24   (4) that is carried out by the Federal Government, or by a State or local

2

1　government with Federal funds, the government shall consider, on the

2　same basis as other nongovernmental organizations, religious organi-

3　zations to provide the assistance under the program, if the program is

4　implemented in a manner that is consistent with the Establishment

5　Clause and the Free Exercise Clause of the first amendment to the

6　Constitution.

7　　　　'(B) DISCRIMINATION PROHIBITED—Neither the Fed-

8　eral Government nor a State or local government receiving funds

9　under a program described in paragraph (4) shall discriminate against

10　an organization that provides assistance under, or applies to provide

11　assistance under, such program, on the basis that the organization has

12　a religious character.

13　　　　'(2) FUNDS NOT AID TO RELIGION—Federal, State, or local

14　government funds or other assistance that is received by a religious or-

15　ganization for the provision of services under this section constitutes

16　aid to individuals and families in need, the ultimate beneficiaries of

17　such services, and not aid to the religious organization.

18　　　　'(3) FUNDS NOT ENDORSEMENT OF RELIGION—The

19　receipt by a religious organization of Federal, State, or local govern-

20　ment funds or other assistance under this section is not and should not

21　be perceived as an endorsement by the government of religion or the

22　organization's religious beliefs or practices.

23　　　　'(4) PROGRAMS—For purposes of this section, a program is

24　described in this paragraph—

25　　　　　　'(A) if it involves activities carried out using Federal funds—

26　　　　　　　　'(i) related to the prevention and treatment of juvenile

27　delinquency and the improvement of the juvenile justice system, in-

28　cluding programs funded under the Juvenile Justice and Delinquency

29　Prevention Act of 1974 (42 U.S.C. 5601 et seq.);

30　　　　　　　　'(ii) related to the prevention of crime, including pro-

31　grams funded under title I of the Omnibus Crime Control and Safe

32　Streets Act of 1968 (42 U.S.C. 3701 et seq.);

3

1   '(iii) under the Federal housing laws;

2   '(iv) under title I of the Workforce Investment Act of 1998

3 (29 U.S.C. 2801 et seq.)

4   '(v) under the Older Americans Act of 1965 (42 U.S.C.

5 3001 et seq.);

6   '(vi) under the Child Care Development Block Grant Act

7 of 1990 (42 U.S.C. 9858 et seq.);

8   '(vii) under the Community Development Block Grant

9 Program established under title I of the Housing and Community

10 Development Act of 1974 (42 U.S.C. 5301 et seq.);

11   '(viii) related to the intervention in and prevention of

12 domestic violence;

13   '(ix) related to hunger relief activities; or

14   '(x) under the Job Access and Reverse Commute grant

15 program established under section 3037 of the Federal Transit Act of

16 1998 (49 U.S.C. 5309 note); or

17   '(B)(i) if it involves activities to assist students in obtaining

18 the recognized equivalents of secondary school diplomas and activities

19 relating to non-school-hours programs; and

20   '(ii) except as provided in subparagraph (A) and clause (i),

21 does not include activities carried out under Federal programs provid-

22 ing education to children eligible to attend elementary schools or sec-

23 ondary schools, as defined in section 14101 of the Elementary and

24 Secondary Education Act of 1965 (20 U.S.C. 8801).

25   '(d) ORGANIZATIONAL CHARACTER AND AUTONOMY—

26   '(1) IN GENERAL—A religious organization that provides as-

27 sistance under a program described in subsection (c)(4) shall retain its

28 autonomy from Federal, State, and local governments, including such

29 organization's control over the definition, development, practice, and

30 expression of its religious beliefs.

31   '(2) ADDITIONAL SAFEGUARDS—Neither the Federal

32 Government nor a State or local government shall require a religious

4

1 organization in order to be eligible to provide assistance under a pro-

2 gram described in subsection (c)(4)—

3   '(A) to alter its form of internal governance; or

4   '(B) to remove religious art, icons, scripture, or other sym-

5 bols because they are religious.

6   '(e) EMPLOYMENT PRACTICES—

7   '(1) IN GENERAL—In order to aid in the preservation of its

8 religious character, a religious organization that provides assistance

9 under a program described in subsection (c)(4) may, notwithstanding

10 any other provision of law, require that its employees adhere to the

11 religious practices of the organization.

12   '(2) TITLE VII EXEMPTION—The exemption of a religious or-

13 ganization provided under section 702 or 703(e)(2) of the Civil Rights

14 Act of 1964 (42 U.S.C. 2000e-1, 2000e-2(e)(2)) regarding employment

15 practices shall not be affected by the religious organization's provision

16 of assistance under, or receipt of funds from, a program described in

17 subsection (c)(4).

18   '(3) EFFECT ON OTHER LAWS—Nothing in this section al-

19 ters the duty of a religious organization to comply with the nondis-

20 crimination provisions in title VI of the Civil Rights Act of 1964 (42

21 U.S.C. 2000d et seq.) (prohibiting discrimination on the basis of race,

22 color, and national origin), title IX of the Education Amendments of

23 1972 (20 U.S.C. 1681-1686) (prohibiting discrimination in educational

24 institutions on the basis of sex and visual impairment), section 504 of

25 the Rehabilitation Act of 1973 (29 U.S.C. 794) (prohibiting discrimina-

26 tion against otherwise qualified disabled individuals), and the Age

27 Discrimination Act of 1975 (42 U.S.C. 6101-6107) (prohibiting dis-

28 crimination on the basis of age).

29   '(f) RIGHTS OF BENEFICIARIES OF ASSISTANCE—

30   '(1) IN GENERAL—If an individual described in paragraph (3)

31 has an objection to the religious character of the organization from

32 which the individual receives, or would receive, assistance funded

5

1   under any program described in subsection (c)(4), the appropriate

2   Federal, State, or local governmental entity shall provide to such indi-

3   vidual (if otherwise eligible for such assistance) within a reasonable

4   period of time after the date of such objection, assistance that—

5   '(A) is an alternative, including a nonreligious alternative,

6   that is accessible to the individual; and

7   '(B) has a value that is not less than the value of the assis-

8   tance that the individual would have received from such organization.

9   '(2) NOTICE—The appropriate Federal, State, or local govern-

10 mental entity shall guarantee that notice is provided to the individu-

11 als described in paragraph (3) of the rights of such individuals under

12 this section.

13   '(3) INDIVIDUAL DESCRIBED—An individual described in

14 this paragraph is an individual who receives or applies for assistance

15 under a program described in subsection (c)(4).

16   '(g) NONDISCRIMINATION AGAINST BENEFICIARIES—

17   '(1) GRANTS AND CONTRACTS—A religious organization

18 providing assistance through a grant or contract under a program de-

19 scribed in subsection (c)(4) shall not discriminate, in carrying out the

20 program, against an individual described in subsection (f)(3)on the

21 basis of religion, a religious belief, or a refusal to hold a religious

22 belief.

23   '(2) INDIRECT FORMS OF DISBURSEMENT—A religious

24 organization providing assistance through a voucher, certificate, or

25 other form of indirect disbursement under a program described in sub-

26 section (c)(4) shall not discriminate, in carrying out the program,

27 against an individual described in subsection (f)(3) on the basis of re-

28 ligion, a religious belief, or a refusal to hold a religious belief.

29   '(h) ACCOUNTABILITY—

30   '(1) IN GENERAL—Except as provided in paragraph (2), a re-

31 ligious organization providing assistance under any program de-

32 scribed in subsection (c)(4) shall be subject to the same regulations as

6

1 other nongovernmental organizations to account in accord with gener-

2 ally accepted accounting principles for the use of such funds provided

3 under such program.

4   '(2) LIMITED AUDIT—Such organization shall segregate gov-

5 ernment funds provided under such program into a separate account

6 or accounts. Only the government funds shall be subject to audit by

7 the government.

8   '(i) LIMITATIONS ON USE OF FUNDS FOR CERTAIN PUR-

9 POSES—No funds provided through a grant or contract to a religious

10 organization to provide assistance under any program described in

11 subsection (c)(4) shall be expended for sectarian worship, instruction,

12 or proselytization. A certificate shall be signed by such organizations

13 and filed with the government agency that disbursed the funds that

14 gives assurance the organization will comply with this subsection.

15   '(j) EFFECT ON STATE AND LOCAL FUNDS—If a State or

16 local government contributes State or local funds to carry out a pro-

17 gram described in subsection (c)(4), the State or local government may

18 segregate the State or local funds from the Federal funds provided to

19 carry out the program or may commingle the State or local funds with

20 the Federal funds. If the State or local government commingles the

21 State or local funds, the provisions of this section shall apply to the

22 commingled funds in the same manner, and to the same extent, as the

23 provisions apply to the Federal funds.

24   '(k) TREATMENT OF INTERMEDIATE CONTRACTORS—If a

25 nongovernmental organization (referred to in this subsection as an 'in-

26 termediate contractor'), acting under a contract or other agreement

27 with the Federal Government or a State or local government, is given

28 the authority under the contract or agreement to select nongovern-

29 mental organizations to provide assistance under the programs de-

30 scribed in subsection (c)(4), the intermediate contractor shall have the

31 same duties under this section as the government when selecting or

32 otherwise dealing with subcontractors, but the intermediate contrac-

7

1   tor, if it is a religious organization, shall retain all other rights of a re-

2   ligious organization under this section.

3   '(l) COMPLIANCE—A party alleging that the rights of the party

4   under this section have been violated by a State or local government

5   may bring a civil action pursuant to section 1979 against the official or

6   government agency that has allegedly committed such violation. A

7   party alleging that the rights of the party under this section have been

8   violated by the Federal Government may bring a civil action for ap-

9   propriate relief in Federal district court against the official or govern-

10 ment agency that has allegedly committed such violation.'

Bush Expected to Announce Effort to Expand 'Charitable Choice'

By David Nather

If religious conservatives do not think President Bush seemed sufficiently committed to school vouchers when he announced his education proposals in the first week of his presidency, they may be happier with the theme of his second week: faith-based social action.

Aides say that during the week of Jan. 29, Bush will announce plans to make good on a campaign pledge to direct more federal aid to religious organizations, charities and community groups that provide social services. The idea, Bush said during the 2000 campaign, is to unleash "armies of compassion."

If he is successful, Bush could help Congress redefine the way the federal government runs its social safety net by using a conservative approach to advance liberal goals. He could also invite greater scrutiny from congressional skeptics and legal challenges on such issues as employment discrimination and the separation of church and state.

"I think [Bush] is going to have a much bigger battle on his hands than we have ever seen on charitable choice," Barry W. Lynn, executive director of Americans United for Separation of Church and State, said Jan. 24. "There is now a bigger group of people who understand the issue much more clearly."

"Charitable choice"—providing federal aid to faith-based social programs without requiring the sponsoring organizations to abandon their religious message—is not a new issue for Congress. Many religious organizations already receive federal funds for welfare-to-work programs, and legislation (PL 106-554) enacted last year allows religion-based drug treatment programs to qualify for federal aid.

Bush wants to go much further. Aides say he will expand his campaign pledge to apply charitable choice to every federal program that allows private groups to provide social services.

That could open the door for religious groups to compete for funds to pay for everything from literacy programs and violence prevention in the schools to public health, housing, and "fatherhood" programs that promote marriage and teach parenting skills. All were the subjects of bills introduced in the 106th Congress, when charitable choice was being promoted on several fronts.

To underscore his belief in charitable choice, Bush is expected to create an Office of Faith-Based Action at the White House. It would serve as a clearinghouse for the initiatives and suggest ways to rewrite regulations that prevent religious groups from participating in federal programs.

Former Indianapolis Mayor Stephen Goldsmith, who served as a Bush domestic policy adviser during the campaign, is the front-runner to head the office, according to congressional sources.

New Tax Incentives

To encourage people to give money to faith-based groups, Bush wants to create new tax incentives, at an estimated cost of $8 billion in the first year. During the 2000 campaign, for example, he proposed allowing taxpayers to deduct their charitable contributions even if they do not itemize their returns. Only 30 percent of Americans now itemize, according to campaign estimates.

Bush will probably find wide support for such tax incentives, though their price tag is certain to be debated. The real issue, and the one that could consume a lot of floor time in Congress, is whether the federal government should be subsidizing religious groups at all.

From *CQ Weekly,* January 27, 2001.

To supporters of faith-based action, Bush's proposals will be an attractive package that could go a long way toward shoring up his support among religious conservatives if he ultimately has to drop school vouchers from his education bill.

Support for the idea of faith-based action is not limited to religious conservatives. Democratic presidential candidate Al Gore talked it up on the campaign trail, as did his running mate, Sen. Joseph I. Lieberman of Connecticut.

"I think the goal is, No. 1, to address the social needs, but No. 2, to revive civil society," Marvin Olasky, a Bush adviser on faith-based action and a senior fellow at the Acton Institute for the Study of Religion and Liberty, a libertarian think tank, said Jan. 24.

To congressional critics, however, it is not that simple. In the House, Robert C. Scott, D-Va., has complained that subsidizing groups without requiring them to comply with federal non-discrimination laws means they could refuse to hire people who disagreed with their religious views.

Scott's concerns provoked a surprisingly strong uprising last year against a child support bill (HR 4678) that would have subsidized faith-based fatherhood programs. He complained that the measure's charitable-choice language could encourage "religious bigotry."

And a charitable-choice provision that would have funded faith-based reading programs was quietly dropped from last year's reauthorization of the Even Start family literacy program.

If Bush gets his way on a broad expansion of charitable choice, any legal challenges will likely be defended by the man who fought in the Senate last year for the broadest possible expansion of charitable choice: Attorney General-designate John Ashcroft.

Charitable-Choice Supporters Put Faith in Court's Judgment

By Elizabeth A. Palmer

True to its name, Faith Works of Milwaukee mixes spirituality with the education and job placement services that Congress helps it offer to drug-addicted fathers who are intent on righting themselves for the sake of their children.

Faith Works' anti-addiction 12-step program is similar to the one Alcoholics Anonymous uses. For advocates of a greater partnership between government and the faith-based community, this small program operating out of an old convent is a shining example of the benefits of using government money to help pay for social programs with a religious flavor.

But it is just that mix of government money and religion that has led critics to challenge the program in court. Observers in and out of Congress are waiting to see whether this program and others like it—which would multiply under President George W. Bush's faith-based initiative—violate the Constitution's separation of church and state.

The answer to that question will weigh heavily on Capitol Hill as lawmakers move to expand these programs under Bush's plan. The suit involving Faith Works, brought by the Freedom From Religion Foundation, could be decided in a Wisconsin federal court by this summer, but observers agree the final word is going to have to come from the Supreme Court. And in recent years, the high court has become harder to predict on questions of separating church and state.

"It's very difficult constitutionally, but there's no question it can be done," said Senate Judiciary Committee Chairman Orrin G. Hatch, R-Utah.

Faith Works has an annual budget of just over $600,000, two-thirds of which comes from government welfare funds. While it has not been around long enough to have established its own performance record, a New York City program upon which the Milwaukee Faith Works is based, claims 8 of 10 clients have remained sober.

Congress cleared the way for Faith Works to get federal support when it added "charitable choice" funding provisions to the 1996 welfare overhaul, and now Bush is moving to build on that by adding to the list of social programs that faith-based groups can perform with federal money.

The Freedom From Religion Foundation wants the court to prohibit further government funding for Faith Works and other programs by finding it in violation of the establishment clause of the Constitution, which says, "Congress shall make no law respecting an establishment of religion or prohibiting the free exercise thereof . . ."

The Supreme Court has struggled for more than 50 years with just what the establishment clause means. While the court has drawn some firm boundaries—forbidding compulsory prayer in public schools, for example—the rules regulating other interactions between government and religion, especially those involving government money, are constantly evolving.

In recent years, the court has sharply split on religious issues, making case-by-case predictions difficult. But the trend appears to be toward allowing some government funding for religious organizations similar to the charitable-choice model.

"It's right at the cusp of where the court is," said Marc D. Stern, a lawyer for the American Jewish Congress.

The court has not ruled on any cases directly analogous to charitable choice because most funding questions it has considered have dealt with government aid and religious schools.

From *CQ Weekly*, March 3, 2001.

Last year, for example, the court ruled 6-3 in favor of a government program that provided computers and other equipment to religious schools. But while the decision might be heartening to those who support charitable choice, the lengthy opinion also showed a court sharply splintered on the core issues.

It is not clear that a majority could be assembled in support of a charitable-choice program.

Bush proposes expanding the range of programs that can receive funding by using the charitable-choice authority to include after school programs, maternity group homes, literacy programs, and those aimed at helping prisoners and their children.

Bush also established an Office of Faith-Based and Community Initiatives within the White House that is charged with eliminating some of the barriers to participation for religious organizations.

"Federal, state and local governments have often acted as if the law banishes religious providers and mandates rigid secularism instead of simple volunteerism, evenhandedness and neutrality," said Bush. He said his goal "is equal opportunity for such groups, a level playing field, a fair chance for them to participate when their programs are successful."

But opponents said his plan steps too far over the line. "The president appears to believe that the government should use religion to solve all of the nation's social problems," said the Rev. Barry W. Lynn, executive director of Americans United for Separation of Church and State. "This approach strikes at the heart of the religious freedoms guaranteed by the First Amendment."

The Faith Works case is not the only one making its way through the system. The American Jewish Congress challenged a Texas program in a suit dismissed earlier this year by a federal judge, though the group might appeal. The group has also filed suit against a program in California under which $5 million was set aside strictly for faith-based organizations.

"What you will not see is a global challenge to the notion of funding religious organizations," Stern said.

Instead, his group and others plan on "sort of setting the outer limits of what's permissible [by] picking the very worst examples."

The first charitable-choice program enacted by Congress was included in the 1996 overhaul of the welfare system (PL 104-193) and allows faith-based groups to compete for funding from the Temporary Assistance for Needy Families program. This is the program through which Faith Works got its government money.

In the 1998 Community Services Block Grant Program (PL 105-285), a charitable-choice provision allows religious groups to compete for grant funds. Then, in the Children's Health Act (PL 106-310) and the Community Renewal Tax Relief Act of 2000 (PL 106-554) faith-based groups were authorized to apply for drug-abuse and treatment grant programs.

Surfacing in Congress

Elements of the Bush plan to expand charitable choice are beginning to surface in Congress. Later this month, the Senate Health, Education, Labor and Pensions Committee is likely to examine its reauthorization of elementary education programs. In it, the committee may choose to include the Bush proposal to allow charitable choice to apply for funding for after-school programs.

The education plan is expected to move quickly through Congress, and little opposition has formed to the charitable-choice element. It is not clear when Bush's other faith-based proposals might move.

While the four existing charitable-choice provisions differ in their details, all are designed to allow religious organizations to compete for federal money without requiring that they lose their religious

continues

orientation or character. The groups, for example, do not have to remove visible symbols of their religious beliefs from areas where they would conduct the program.

They also are exempt from some federal employment discrimination regulations and can confine their hiring to those who support their beliefs.

Most of the charitable-choice programs—those enacted and those proposed by Bush—cannot get federal money unless the service they offer is available from a non-religious group.

Douglas Laycock, a law professor at the University of Texas School of Law in Austin, said that could prove to be the plan's biggest obstacle because many rural areas cannot afford to sustain duplicate social service programs.

"The problem is in the details," he said. "In the big picture, this is fine constitutionally."

Laycock noted that religious organizations have been getting government money for decades, from Catholic hospitals to reimbursements for stays by the homeless at religious-run shelters.

Charitable-choice programs also must be managed in a manner consistent with the establishment clause, a requirement Nathan Diament, director of the Institute for Public Affairs for the Union of Orthodox Jewish Congregations of America, characterized as: "Bring on the lawsuits and let's figure this out."

President Bill Clinton sought to maintain a divide between church and state, even as he signed the laws creating charitable choice. In 1998, Clinton attached a note to the reauthorization of the Community Services Block Grant declaring, "I construe the Act as forbidding the funding of pervasively sectarian organizations."

The Supreme Court previously had held that pervasively sectarian or purely religious organizations could not be eligible for government funding, but that is a position from which a conflicted court seems to be retreating.

Court Evolving

The schism within the court on the issue of government aid to religious organizations was on full display in its 2000 decision, *Mitchell v. Helms.*

Though the decision upheld a federal program that provided computers and other aid to private, mostly religious, schools in Louisiana, the opinion was striking because of the sharp disagreements between justices, even those who agreed on the outcome.

The decision, issued with three justices writing opinions, showed that on the matter of government support of religious organizations, the court is divided between what Barbara A. Perry, a government professor at Sweet Briar College in Virginia, calls the "separationists" and "accommodationists."

For much of the last century, the separationist wing—which holds that government should be entirely removed from religion—controlled the court on most religious issues. That position is currently espoused by the more liberal wing of the court, Justices John Paul Stevens, David H. Souter, Ruth Bader Ginsburg, and sometimes Stephen G. Breyer.

The 1971 decision, *Lemon v. Kurtzman,* in which the court set out a three-pronged test to determine whether government aid to a religious organization was constitutional, was a key success for the separationists and provided the blueprint for evaluating most government aid cases almost up to the *Mitchell* case in 2000.

Now, the accommodationist wing, which is comfortable with government connections to religion as long as the government is neutral on the religion, appears to be ascending. Four conservative justices make up this camp: Chief Justice William H. Rehnquist, Antonin Scalia, Anthony M. Kennedy and Clarence Thomas.

They believe it is important "not to penalize religion by keeping government money out of it," said Perry.

Supporters of charitable choice believe the accommodationists would likely support these programs. But in order to win a majority they would have to win over the woman in the middle—Justice Sandra Day O'Connor.

As is true in so many areas, O'Connor is the key, providing a deciding vote on a case-by-case basis and keeping neither side from winning clear decisions on the issue. She sided with the separationists in the 2000 decision, *Santa Fe Independent School District v. Jane Doe* that prohibited student-led prayer at public school football games, but was on the side of the accommodationists when it came to providing government aid to private, religious schools in *Mitchell*.

It is clear from the language used by the Bush team in announcing its proposal that they are hoping to appeal to the four conservative justices who are trying to move the court toward allowing more access to federal funds for religious organizations.

"Government should welcome these groups to apply for funds, not discriminate against them," Bush said when addressing Congress on Feb. 27.

Justice Thomas wrote for the four-member plurality in *Mitchell*. "We have consistently turned to the principal of neutrality, upholding aid that is offered to a broad range of groups or persons without regard to their religion."

But O'Connor may be difficult to persuade. She wrote her own opinion in the *Mitchell* case, distancing herself from the accommodationists even as she voted with them.

"I write separately because, in my view, the plurality announces a rule of unprecedented breadth for the evaluation of Establishment Clause challenges to government school aid . . . we have never held that a government aid program passes constitutional muster solely because of the neutral criteria it employs as a basis for distributing aid."

And, she warned, "the plurality opinion foreshadows the approval of direct monetary subsidies to religious organizations, even when they use the money to advance their religious objectives," something O'Connor appeared to be signalling that she would find unconstitutional.

O'Connor did not dispute Thomas' point that the court should not assume government aid to pervasively religious groups is unconstitutional.

"[T]he religious nature of the recipient should not matter to the constitutional analysis, so long as the recipient adequately furthers the government's secular purpose," wrote Thomas. "In short, nothing in the Establishment Clause requires the exclusion of pervasively sectarian schools from otherwise permissible aid programs and other doctrines of this Court bar it."

Faith-Based Initiatives

By Sarah Glazer

The Issues

John Reese says he has finally kicked his 12-year cocaine habit. For that he thanks Teen Challenge, a Christian rehab program, the only one of the five treatment programs he tried that worked for him. The others, including Alcoholics Anonymous, failed to make an impact, according to Reese, 38, because they "aimed at the head but not the heart."

He credits the program with saving his marriage and ending the cycle of crimes he committed to feed his habit. Drug-free since last December, he works as a maintenance assistant at the Teen Challenge program in Brooklyn, N.Y., and is studying for the ministry.

"Until I came to terms with sin in my life, I would continually relapse," Reese says. Although he was not particularly religious before entering Teen Challenge, Reese, like other successful graduates, attributes the program's success to "the Jesus factor."

President Bush has praised Teen Challenge as an example of the religious groups he wants to make eligible for federal funding as part of his new faith-based initiative. Arguing that religious groups may be more successful than government bureaucracies in tackling intractable social problems, Bush has initiated a multipronged effort to allow churches and other faith-based groups to apply for federal grants to deliver a wide range of social services. [1]

But many questions have been raised about Teen Challenge, and many go to the heart of Bush's ini-

From *The CQ Researcher*, May 4, 2001.

The Salvation Army mixes a Christian message with its wide array of community services. It has received federal funds since its founding in the late 19th century as a missionary group.

Salvation Army

tiative: Should programs like Teen Challenge, which rely entirely on religious instructors rather than trained addiction counselors, receive taxpayers' dollars? And will the funding of Christian programs deprive social-service recipients of non-religious alternatives? (*See story, p. 60.*)

Then there's the ultimate constitutional conundrum: If the "Jesus factor" is what works, how can the government support the program without violating the constitutional prohibition against promoting an individual group's religion?

Civil libertarians argue that any program that insists on acceptance of Christianity as part of its treatment, like Teen Challenge, should be barred from government support. The First Amendment is supposed to prevent the government from favoring one religion over another, says Rep. Robert C. Scott, D-Va., a leading opponent of Bush's initiative. "Which re-

ligious groups should get federal money to convert people to their religion?" he asks.

Scott envisions a new form of religious pork barrel as different faiths jockey for federal funds and for local politicians' favor. "Who gets to feed at the public trough?" he asks. "You're talking about billions of dollars."

Until 1996, religious groups couldn't receive federal money unless they either set up a secular arm to deliver government-funded services or delivered secular services separately from their religious mission. But the little-noticed "charitable choice" provision of the 1996 Welfare Reform Act and three other laws signed by President Bill Clinton lowered the traditional wall between church and state. [2] Authored by then-Sen. John Ashcroft, R-Mo., now U.S. attorney general, charitable choice permits religious groups to apply directly for federal funds for welfare-to-work and drug treatment programs. However, such groups may not use federal funds for worship, conversion or religious instruction.

Concerned about the constitutional questions, the Clinton administration did little to promote the participation of religious groups. [3] By contrast, the budget proposed by the Bush White House would expand the types of social-service programs covered to include mentoring prisoners' children, helping fathers leave welfare and providing shelter for teen mothers.

The Bush administration is also supporting a House Republican bill to open nine additional programs — including juvenile delinquency prevention programs, senior citizens programs and housing grants — to direct bidding from religious groups. Because of its wide scope, the legislation will have to win the approval of numerous committees before reaching the floor, and the timetable for floor action is uncertain.

The new chief of the White House Office of Faith-Based and Community Initiatives, John J. DiIulio Jr., argues that the government's traditional reliance on secular, nonprofit organizations to carry out its social service agenda has failed.

"We have myriad programs for after-school literacy, and yet we have millions of children going through those programs and little evidence anyone ends up reading at or near grade level," he says. "We have spent scores of billions on housing rehab programs, and a third of the housing stock remains falling down. We have welfare-to-work programs that often succeed in getting none of their clients into long-term, living-wage jobs."

African-American and Latino churches are often the only local institutions in inner-city neighborhoods providing essential services like day care or job training, argues DiIulio, who became a champion of several inner-city ministers while studying their work as a social scientist at the University of Pennsylvania. He contrasts their holistic work with government programs that deal with disadvantaged youths one problem at a time — truancy, criminal violations, learning problems.

"The kid is a soul, a spirit, a body, an emotional self and a lived self," DiIulio says. "And the difference [in a faith-based organization] is the kid is a whole person, and the people providing the services are there so they can hook up with probation and the school and follow the kid through."

A recent poll illustrates the tension between supporting religious groups and crossing the line to government-supported religion. While the survey found broad public support for allowing religiously affiliated charitable organizations to apply for government funding, support drops off sharply if the groups encourage re-ligious conversion. And a majority of respondents worried the initiative would interfere with the separation between church and state. [4]

That tension reflects a unique American paradox, says Alan Wolfe, director of the Boisi Center for Religion and American Public Life at Boston College and author of *Moral Freedom*, a new book that deals with the issue. Americans are deeply religious, Wolfe says, but they have doubts about sects — as indicated by negative attitudes the poll found toward public funding of Scientologists and other sects — and they have reservations about "in-your-face" evangelism.

As Wolfe sees the problem, religious groups typically embrace a specific religious viewpoint. Teen Challenge, for example, espouses the view that Jesus Christ replaces the emptiness in the soul formerly filled by drugs. To support that approach, the government would have to support a specific religious viewpoint — which is what the Constitution appears to ban, Wolfe observes. "Exactly what makes the program work is what makes it unconstitutional," he says.

In addition, by law, religious institutions are allowed to discriminate on religious grounds in hiring so they can hire someone of their own faith. Bush's initiative would extend the exemption to religious groups even when they receive federal funds. Supporters of the provision argue the discrimination exemption is essential if religious groups are to preserve their identity.

Opponents say charitable choice gives carte blanche to groups to discriminate against employees on the basis of religious beliefs, which could then extend to race (some evangelical Christians, for example, oppose interracial dating) or sexual orientation (some religions view homosexuality as a sin).

Civil liberties groups are primed to challenge the hiring exemption in court. "The first call we get from anyone discriminated against on those grounds we would be happy to help them out," says Barry Lynn, executive director of Americans United for Separation of Church and State.

To Rep. Scott, an African-American, charitable choice provides nothing more than "the right to discriminate and the right to advance your religion."

Responding to DiIulio's concerns about inner-city blacks, Scott asks, "Why should we have to sell off our civil rights in order for you to spend money in the inner city?" He suggests that small black churches would be better served if the government offered to help them write grants under existing federal contracting rules. Under charitable choice, Scott predicts, "Those little churches are no more likely to get the money than they were before."

Several observers worry that the federal government could end up supporting fringe cults or religious groups that promote hate. Televangelist Pat Robertson has warned the initiative could open a "Pandora's box" by making funds available to Scientologists, the Nation of Islam or religious cults that employ "brainwashing techniques." [5]

The proposal has created strange bedfellows: Some evangelical Christians have sided with some African-American churches in supporting the proposal, while Baptist denominations that oppose the government's infringement on religion find themselves in the same camp with the American Civil Liberties Union (ACLU), which opposes any breach in the wall between church and state. Recently, labor groups came out against the proposal because it permits hiring discrimination. [6]

If there is a middle ground where liberals can meet conservatives from the faith community, it may be the idea that people need personal mentoring and some kind of inner transformation (an old conservative idea) as well as material help (the 1960s anti-poverty premise) to get out of poverty. Two dozen leading liberals, conservatives and religious leaders sent a consensus statement to the White House on April 27 supporting government assistance to faith-based groups. * The signers include John Castellani, president of Teen Challenge, and Harris Wofford, President John F. Kennedy's special assistant on civil rights and former head of the Corps for National Service under President Clinton.

"People who are inspired by their faith can add the sense of urgency that so many of these problems require," Wofford says, noting that 5,000 Americorps volunteers a year were assigned to faith-based programs, which were selected because they were often considered the best programs helping people in a community.

Although a majority of both houses approved charitable choice provisions in the last Congress, last week was the first time hearings have been held on the provisions. The additional scrutiny will shine a spotlight on the constitutional objections, which got little attention in the larger welfare reform debate in 1996. It may also bring new attention to the reality that millions of dollars in federal funds already go to religious groups like the Salvation Army, which mixes Christianity with its services for the homeless. [7]

As lawmakers and social-service providers debate constitutional and other questions about the initiative, these are some of the questions they are asking:

---

* The Consensus Group was organized by Search for Common Ground, USA.

Can religious groups provide social services more effectively than government agencies and secular groups?

Marvin Olasky's 1992 book, *The Tragedy of American Compassion*, is often cited as an influential source for President Bush's brand of "compassionate conservatism." Olasky, editor of the weekly Christian news magazine *World*, argues that the Great Society programs of the 1960s encouraged the poor to develop a sense of entitlement toward their welfare benefits rather than a sense of personal responsibility. He con-

John J. DiIulio Jr., head of the new White House Office of Faith-Based and Community Initiatives, argues that the government's traditional reliance on secular organizations to deliver social services has failed.

trasts the 1960s, when welfare rolls exploded, with the 1890s, when religious charities often required work in return for a handout.

Olasky argues that religious groups today are more successful at helping people out of poverty than government programs because they, like the 19th-century charities, challenge individuals to change from within.

"Isn't it time that we start managing by results, even if that means returning social services to those private and religious institutions that emphasize challenging compassion?" Olasky asked. [8]

Olasky's journalistic accounts claimed high success rates for religious groups among those they help, but there's virtually no social science evidence that they do better than non-religious groups. Similarly, writing of Teen Challenge and the Salvation Army last fall, DiIulio noted, "[W]e do not really know whether these faith-based programs or others like them outperform their secular counterparts, how they compare to one another or whether in any case it is the 'faith' in 'faith-based' that mainly determines any observed differences in outcomes." [9]

So far, the closest social scientists have come to an answer has been in the study of church attendance and juvenile delinquency. Recent University of Pennsylvania studies found that black youths from crime-ridden neighborhoods who attend church regularly are less likely to commit violent crime or use drugs than their peers. [10] But it's not clear if that's because the kinds of teens who attend churches already come from more law-abiding and less troubled families.

"Kids in church are choosing to be there. It's very likely to be a different kind of kid," says Mark Chaves, a sociologist at the University of Arizona. "Claims that we know these [faith-based organizations] are better are not justified."

In what may be the first systematic comparison to date, David Reingold, an assistant professor at Indiana University's School of Environmental and Public Affairs, compared how faith-based and secular groups in Indiana rated their effectiveness in providing social services. Faith-based groups rate themselves less effective than secular

AP Photo/Dennis Cook

Kicking Addiction at Teen Challenge

Seated in a semicircle, Bibles on their desks, a dozen men in a Brooklyn basement are preparing to visit local churches, where they will describe how their newly found faith in Jesus Christ is helping them to kick lives of addiction.

The men are all residents of Teen Challenge, a non-denominational Christian program that treats about 3,000 addicts each year at 150 drug rehabilitation centers nationwide. [1] Because the program does not use state-licensed addiction counselors, the Brooklyn branch is ineligible for state funding and relies entirely on private donations to provide free, yearlong residential treatment to each of its 45 men and women. However, that could all change under President George W. Bush's proposal to allow religious groups to apply for federal drug treatment funds under his proposed Faith-Based Initiative plan.

Many question whether taxpayers' dollars should fund such programs, in which the religious message is inextricable from the drug counseling — as it clearly is in this class. Prepping the students for their presentations, the teacher instructs, "You want to elevate Christ."

His students respond in the same vernacular. "When people read of the pain and suffering Jesus Christ went through, [they'll realize that] most of us have been there: When you've got lots of years of bondage, hating that drink but knowing you need it," says a neatly dressed red-haired man in a madras shirt. "I've carried my own [cross], man."

His words are greeted by a chorus of "Amens" from the mixed group of African-American, Hispanic and white men, ranging from their 20s to middle-aged. The central message of the program is that addiction is a sin and that accepting Jesus Christ is the solution.

But several express doubts about how they will fare once they leave the program. "My greatest challenge will be when I'm out in the street," says a young man recalling the worldly pull he felt in a recent conversation with an old friend from the streets.

"The temptation will still be there," the instructor answers. "We definitely are weak men, and that's why we need Christ."

When another student laments that drugs have impaired his mental faculties and his ability to memorize Bible verses, the teacher again is encouraging, a quality of the program successful graduates often praise. "It's going to take time. Don't rush it,'" the teacher says.

Work in the kitchen as well as daily prayer are important parts of the therapy for these two former drug abusers at the Teen Challenge program in Brooklyn.

Teen Challenge

Women Confront Abuse

Most of the women at the Brooklyn Teen Challenge women's residence were sexually abused before they began using drugs, says Dave Batty, executive director of the center. Much of the women's counseling focuses on those old and painful issues, he says, adding, "Abuse issues are far more difficult to deal with than heroin addiction."

Although Batty says acceptance of Jesus Christ is the key to the program, when it comes to sexual abuse, he sounds like a mainstream psychologist. Intensive counseling is often necessary before the women can break the habit of turning to illegal drugs, he says.

Phyllis Jones, 48, a 1995 graduate of the program, says sexual abuse by a family member — starting when she was 4 — precipitated her drug use, which began with marijuana at 9 and heroin sniffing at 16. She ran away from another drug rehabilitation program, Odyssey House, in 1992, when she was pregnant with her first child. She recalled one particularly humiliating incident at Odyssey when the staff tied her by the wrist to another addict as they were squired to a medical clinic for prenatal treatment.

"There was a lot of condemnation" for being an addict, she says. "Your self-esteem was always torn down. Here [at Teen Challenge] they told me it was going to be OK." Jones was HIV positive and convinced she was about to

groups when it comes to an elaborate program like helping individuals find and keep a job, he found. But they think they're as effective in more traditional congregational activities like gathering food for the needy. [11]

"It shouldn't be that much of a surprise that faith-based organiza-tions are organized around meeting immediate needs — food pantries as opposed to job training," Reingold says.

die when her sister, a practicing Christian, got her into the Brooklyn Teen Challenge program in 1993.

The religious focus "was real strange at first," Jones says. But the combination of discipline and love from the female staff allowed her to come to terms with her past abuse and the void she had filled with men and drugs, she says. "I always say this is where I was reborn again," she says. At Teen Challenge, "I felt like I was somebody."

Today Jones is a counseler and teacher at Teen Challenge. She recently married and is studying to be a non-denominational minister and to get her license as a state-certified addiction counselor.

Some successful graduates of Teen Challenge say the program resonated with them because they had a religious upbringing. Maria Rodriquez, who was raised Catholic, said other programs failed to help her deal with her alcoholism, which she also says was rooted in a history of sexual abuse. She thinks the other programs failed because they lacked a religious component.

"I was looking for somebody real so I could be free of bondage inside," Rodriguez says. "Now I call God first." Rodriquez has been a house manager and teacher at Teen Challenge for the past six years.

Success Rates Questioned

A 1975 study of Teen Challenge's effectiveness by the National Institute on Drug Abuse (NIDA) found that while some people, like Jones and Rodriquez, thrived on the program's religious component, others were put off by it. "Too much religion" was a main reason cited by the 82 percent who drop out of the program before graduation. Teen Challenge's Web site highlights the study's finding that 67 percent of graduates remain drug-free seven years later. But, the NIDA study found that only 18 percent graduate, which casts doubt on the 67 percent success rate, say addiction experts. [2]

The program's Web site also claims an 86 percent success rate based on a 1995 study completed for a doctoral dissertation at Northwestern University. But that study also fails to count dropouts. According to the Northwestern study, Teen Challenge graduates reported returning to drug use less often than graduates of a hospital drug rehabilitation program, but not less than hospital program graduates who continued attending Alcoholics Anonymous support groups. [3] Critics also note that many drug treatment programs often are sent unwilling addicts by court order, while Teen Challenge selects its clients, choosing those who express an affinity for its religious approach.

Lack of Licensing Questioned

Addiction specialists also are concerned about the lack of licensed counselors at Teen Challenge, particularly in such potentially dangerous situations as detoxification.

"It is anti-intellectual, anti-professional and potentially dangerous to [addicted] patients to presume that all they need is spiritual advice," says Michael Miller, chairman of the public policy committee of the American Society for Addiction Medicine.

But John Castellani, president of Teen Challenge International USA, based in Springfield, Mo., responds that the program routinely sends addicts to detox at local hospitals before they enter Teen Challenge.

Teen Challenge's unlicensed status brought it to the attention of food stamp authorities in Texas. According to Castellani, the state threatened to cancel the food stamps that clients received at a Texas Teen Challenge center, on the grounds the program was unlicensed. However, then-Gov. Bush signed legislation permitting such unlicensed faith-based groups to remain eligible for government assistance.

Nevertheless, some Teen Challenge officials are ambivalent about the possibility of receiving federal funds other than food stamps, since federal law prohibits religious groups from spending federal funds on religious conversion, worship or instruction.

On the one hand, Batty says he would welcome government money for such non-spiritual items as a new sidewalk and new bathrooms for the facility. And, some program aspects that are not religiously oriented might be eligible for federal funding, such as job training, drug prevention programs and preparing students to take the GED (high school equivalency exams).

But, "the spiritual component is the key to our success," says Batty. "We're not willing to give that up just to get government money."

---

[1] Teen Challenge was created in 1961 by David Wilkerson, a Pennsylvania minister working with gang youth in Brooklyn. Today, Teen Challenge accepts addicts and alcoholics who are at least 17 years old; the Brooklyn program mainly treats adults.

[2] Catherine B. Hess, "Research Summation," Teen Challenge Training Center, and "An Evaluation of the Teen Challenge Treatment Program," National Institute on Drug Abuse, 1977.

[3] See Laurie Goodstein, "Church-Based Projects Lack Data on Results," *The New York Times*, April 14, 2001, p. A12 and "Teen Challenge is Proven Answer to the Drug Problem" at www.teenchallenge.com.

Similarly, in a national survey, Chaves found that religious congregations mainly get involved in emergency help — collecting food and clothing or giving temporary shelter to the homeless. [12]

"You sometimes get the impression that people think congregations are more likely to be holistic, more personal, more focused on transformational things, but that doesn't seem to be true," Chaves says. Only about

3 percent of congregations get federal funding, and fewer than 10 percent do personal transformational work, such as mentoring or drug rehabilitation, his study found. [13]

"It's not at all clear congregations would be good at this," Chaves maintains. The Mississippi Faith and Families Program, a state effort often held up as an exemplar to get churches to help women make the transition from welfare to work, "was a total failure," he says. "It was canceled six months after it started because congregations didn't know what to do."

Although DiIulio concedes that the belief that religious programs will outperform comparable programs is a hypothesis, not a "settled fact," he says he's willing to "make the same bet" as believers like Olasky that they will work better. [14]

What drives the confidence behind that bet? DiIulio's answer is the famous Woody Allen observation that "90 percent of life is showing up." In essence, DiIulio argues, black and Latino ministers and their congregational members succeed because they show up — because they live in the pockets of poverty where the neediest live.

"In most cases, these are volunteers who have firsthand knowledge and a personal stake," DiIulio maintains.

In addition, small church programs take a more flexible approach that responds more to an individual's needs than to an impersonal government mandate, DiIulio says. And, echoing Olasky, DiIulio says faith-based programs are more likely to require reciprocity from the people they serve in terms of work or behavior. DiIulio cites the Victory Fellowship, a Christian drug rehabilitation program founded by addict-turned-pastor Freddie Garcia in San Antonio in 1972, which works inside prisons and on the streets with gang members. The program, which puts a heavy emphasis on personal responsibility, makes former prisoners and addicts scrub down pews or wash pots if they violate the program's rules. "Generally in the faith community, a person may have had life troubles, but [the philosophy is] 'Now you're getting help, and you have to give respect in return,' " DiIulio says. "And that works."

African-American ministers may also play a crucial role as intermedi-

> "A lot of what the faith-based initiative is about is trying to clarify the rules. Because the rules have been exceedingly unclear, faith-based groups have been scared to participate in public programs."
>
> — *Michael W. McConnell, constitutional law expert, University of Utah College of Law*

aries between black youth and traditionally estranged institutions like the police, according to Christopher Winship, chairman of Harvard University's sociology department. Winship has studied the work of Eugene Rivers, pastor of the Azusa Christian Community, a Pentecostal church in Boston's impoverished Dorchester section. Rivers was a leading member of a group of ministers who founded the Ten Point Coalition in 1992 to tackle Boston's epidemic of gang-related deaths. DiIulio has often cited Rivers' work with youth as a prime example of what the federal government should fund.

Winship has argued that the Ten Point Coalition played a critical role in Boston's 72 percent drop in homicides between 1992 and 1997 by creating an "umbrella of legitimacy" for the police. Ministers like Rivers, who had previously been vocal critics of police stop-and-frisk tactics in black neighborhoods, began to visit gang members, promising swift retribution from the law if they continued the violence but help with school, jobs and pressure from gangs if they went straight. [15]

Although Winship has not studied the effectiveness of these programs specifically, when it comes to "messy moral issues" like youth violence and teen pregnancy, he suggests, ministers may be able to play a unique role. "Because we have a workable model, we've been able to convince a lot of kids to get out of gang-banging," Winship says.

Winship says he has also been impressed by the role these churches have played in partnership with community health centers, where they address inherently delicate issues like family relationships and sex. Ministers have a "unique moral standing" in their community, he has observed. "Maybe they're in a position to talk to people about the way they live their lives that standard nonprofits do not."

President Bush has been an enthusiastic supporter of ex-Watergate felon Charles W. Colson's Prison Fellowship Ministries. Boosters of the program claim recidivism rates four times lower than for those of prisoners released without its help. [16] But Lynn of Americans United for Separation of Church and State notes it is often the only program a prison offers to help prisoners being released. Its success, Lynn suggests, could be the result of the extra family time obtained for fellowship participants, the fact that they are handpicked for the program or the help they receive in job placement rather than the Christian message.

Similar skepticism has been voiced about the high success rates with addicts claimed by Teen Challenge, which boasts a 67 percent cure rate.

Relatively little is known about the power of spirituality in drug-treatment programs like Alcoholics Anonymous, but community support may be as important as the religious factor, according to Richard K. Fuller, director of clinical and prevention research at the National Institute on Alcohol Abuse and Alcoholism (NIAA). Project Match, the largest such study conducted by NIAA, compared a spiritually oriented addiction-treatment program, Alcoholics Anonymous, to two other standard secular approaches, behavior and motivational enhancement therapy. The percentages rehabilitated were similar for all three treatment methods.

At the same time, addiction experts have expressed concern that counselors at programs like Teen Challenge lack the medical qualifications necessary to deal with detoxification, which can be fatal under some circumstances.

"We're very concerned that any lack of seriousness about this disease — alcohol dependence — as a real medical condition will potentially harm patients," says Geoff Laredo, director of NIAA's Office of Policy, Legislation and Public Liaison. "Would you go in for brain surgery without a qualified neurosurgeon?"

Counters DiIulio: "It's not always the case that certification equals qualification. After two decades of federal, state and local investments, we've seen relatively little evidence of success from even the most highly credentialed therapeutic programs. Many of the people who do that [work] at the grass roots may not have a Ph.D. in psychiatric social work but have themselves been drug addicts — and have no less concrete evidence of success than the professional, get-all-the-degree folks."

DiIulio has stressed repeatedly in public appearances that measurable results will be the new administration's most important criteria in deciding which groups get funded — for example, the number of drug addicts who remain abstinent, the number of children reading at grade level.

But James Q. Wilson, professor emeritus of management and public policy at the University of California at Los Angeles, notes that empirical tests are hard to arrange for small, understaffed activities. [17] Moreover, personal transformation, which is at the core of religion, is hard to measure with traditional statistics. "This is not an activity of which research foundations or schools of public policy know much," Wilson writes, even though, it's "a powerful force" that has shaped nations and cultures. [18]

Does government funding for religious groups violate the separation between church and state required by the Constitution?

The fundamental constitutional question raised by charitable choice is whether its provisions violate the separation between church and state set out by the First Amendment's so-called Establishment Clause: "Congress shall make no law respecting an establishment of religion or prohibiting the free exercise thereof."

At the root of the debate is a disagreement over what the Framers intended. Olasky, an early proponent of funding faith-based organizations, argues that the Framers were trying to prevent the establishment of a state religion, not forbid all state aid to religion. Olasky is part of a wave of evangelical Christians who argue that the nation has gone too far in distancing itself from religion. Similarly, Wilson argues the Framers intended merely to prevent the government from imposing religious practices. [19]

But civil libertarians read the Establishment Clause as prohibiting any government support of religion. Eliot Mincberg, legal director of People for the American Way, is quick to recall James Madison's contention that not three pence of tax money should support any religion. [20]

Supreme Court decisions since the late 1940s have reflected both points of view. In the court's first decisive case, *Everson v. Board of Education of Ewing Township*, the court allowed New Jersey to reimburse parents for bus fare to parochial schools. But the 1947 ruling held, in a phrase borrowed from Thomas Jefferson, that the Establishment Clause erected a "wall of separation" between church and state. High court decisions during the 1970s supported this view (*see p. 68*).

Recent Supreme Court cases appear to be moving away from the principle laid down in earlier cases starting with *Everson* that there should "no direct aid" for religion. In the most recent case, *Mitchell v. Helms*, decided last year, the court declared that it was constitutional for the government to provide computers and other educational equipment to religious as well as public schools. In the closely watched case, four justices embraced the "neutrality" theory, arguing that aid to religious schools was constitutional as long as the aid is distributed even-handedly to religious and non-religious institutions alike according to secular criteria.

However the "neutrality" principle does not represent a majority position on the court. (Two justices said the government can't give aid that is used for religious instruction, and three said the government can't give aid likely to be used for religious instruction.)

"The honest answer is the law is uncertain as to what kind of aid to religious groups is impermissible," says Erwin Chemerinsky, a constitutional expert and professor of law at the University of Southern California (USC).

Chemerinsky thinks charitable choice violates the wall that separates church and state. "I think it will inevitably lead to coercion and to people participating in religions they don't believe in," he says. "I also think charitable choice will be a threat to religion. With government comes government monitoring and government conditions."

Charitable choice provisions in existing law forbid religious groups from using public funds for proselytizing, religious instruction or worship. But civil-liberties groups doubt that restriction could be enforced in practice.

"I've heard John DiIulio say the government can provide the chairs and someone else will provide the Bibles in a welfare-to-work program," Mincberg says. "That kind of mixing, where government is paying part of the cost, is a constitutional problem because it is government helping to promote the religious mission."

Some religious groups have expressed concern that the government would discriminate against minority religions seeking funding and against individual adherents of minority faiths.

Marc Stern, legal director of the American Jewish Congress, says "there's a sense of disquiet" among Jews and concern that the initiative would exclude them from social services, especially where they are few in number.

"In the panhandle of Oklahoma, nobody's going to fund a Jewish program instead of a Baptist program," he says. "This is designed for everybody but small religious groups." The Interfaith Alliance, representing 50 faiths from Christians and Jews to Bahai, opposes the initiative on similar grounds.

Several religious groups oppose charitable choice because they say it would interfere with religion. "We believe religion fares best when left unencumbered by the government," says K. Hollyn Hollman, general counsel for the Baptist Joint Committee on Public Affairs. "Charitable choice says you don't need to separate religious activity from government activity, and we think that causes a threat to the separation of church and state."

Hollman notes that religious organizations already have a constitutional mechanism for receiving state aid for social services — setting up a non-religious nonprofit designated in the Tax Code as a 501c(3). "If the thinking is to allow religious people to be involved, it's unneeded," she says.

But a constitutional expert who supports charitable choice, Michael W. McConnell of the University of Utah College of Law, says the government has sent conflicting signals as to how much religion is allowed in government-funded programs. The Salvation Army, a longtime recipient of federal funds, has not set up a separate secular branch, McConnell notes. Some of its missions have a strongly Christian flavor, while others have been told to tone down the religious element.

"A lot of what the faith-based initiative is about is trying to clarify what the rules are, because the rules have been exceedingly unclear in the past 20-30 years," McConnell says. "As a result, faith-based groups have been at the mercy of changing and conflicting regulations, which has made them scared to participate in public programs."

As a constitutional matter, McConnell sees nothing wrong with government funding of faith-based groups as long as the beneficiaries are not coerced into religious activities and have a non-religious alternative to choose from. "I say it's the separationists who are trying to restrict the range of beneficiaries' choices," he contends. "The First Amendment ought to be interpreted to allow beneficiaries, if they choose, to select religiously oriented programs."

However critics note that while charitable choice provisions require a secular alternative be available, there is no requirement that a drug addict or other government beneficiary be informed that he has such a right.

Less public discussion has been focused on a provision of charitable choice that permits the use of vouchers to obtain social services from a religious group. DiIulio told the Manhattan Institute last month that vouchers might be a solution for a group like Teen Challenge, where religious counseling is inseparable from the drug-addiction treatment. Using vouchers might avoid the constitutional battle awaiting direct grants to religious groups. That's because the Supreme Court has given greater constitutional leeway to public aid received only indirectly by religious institutions (such as through vouchers) than it has to direct aid. [21] The court's decisions suggest that a method like vouchers would be constitutional as long as the voucher recipient is given a genuine choice between religious and non-religious groups.

Members of the evangelical community, including Olasky, prefer vouchers or tax credits to grants, which they see placing unworkable restrictions on a religious group's exercise of its faith. James Q. Wilson recently editorialized in favor of vouchers as permitting a church to help a homeless drug addict "without at the same time denying its own deep beliefs." [22] But vouchers would likely be more helpful for larger, better-known congregations than little urban ones, which might find themselves overlooked by people searching for social services.

Should faith-based groups be allowed to practice religious discrimination in hiring?

Charitable choice provisions exempt religious institutions from the 1964 Civil Rights Act prohibition

Will Churches Do More?

Will churches and other religious organizations expand their role in social services under President George W. Bush's faith-based initiative?

Nationwide, only a handful of large congregations currently deliver most of the faith-based social services, according to a national survey by University of Arizona sociologist Mark Chaves. In fact, the largest 10 percent of churches and synagogues account for more than half of congregational spending on social services, he says. Most of them have already set up separate, secular, nonprofit branches, which traditionally has been required in order for a church to receive federal support, Chaves says.

In light of his findings, Chaves doubts that many new churches will take advantage of new "charitable choice" laws designed to help churches apply for federal grants to deliver social services. Under the new laws churches are not required to set up separate social service entities in order to receive public aid.

But University of Pennsylvania associate professor of social work Ram Cnaan thinks many churches — especially in urban centers — will take advantage of the new rules. He surveyed 113 urban congregations in six cities and discovered an untapped well of social services, particularly in inner-city ministries. In Philadelphia, for instance, Cnaan found that black congregations were more likely than white congregations to offer the kinds of services Bush has targeted in his faith-based initiative: mentoring at-risk youth, providing child care and health education, tutoring adults and training young people to use computers. [1]

The aggregate annual value of social services contributed by Philadelphia congregations is estimated at $230 million, Cnaan found, with most of the help going to "unchurched" neighborhood youth. Cnaan found that four times as many non-members as congregation members receive services, ranging from feeding programs to teen recreation programs. [2]

Cnaan's findings also suggest that more churches would seek government grants if they knew about charitable choice. Cnaan found in a recent survey that most clergy had never heard of charitable choice, but 60 percent said they were interested in receiving federal funds for their social service programs.

In fact, on March 31, some 450 predominantly African-American Philadelphia clergy attended a meeting Cnaan helped organize to offer help in writing federal grant applications. "This clearly shows they're willing to do more if given a chance," Cnaan says.

Another sign of untapped potential cited by Cnaan is the recent outpouring of interest in congregations partnering with secular nonprofits. For instance, about 550 volunteers recently answered the call of Philadelphia congregations seeking mentors for prisoners' children, he says. Big Brothers/Big Sisters trained and then matched the volunteers to inmates' children, considered one of the most at-risk populations in the United States.

"We went and knocked on doors and got about 50 congregations to give us people," says Cnaan, who called it an enormous outpouring for one city.

The Rev. Eugene Rivers, a strong supporter of the Bush initiative, says his non-denominational church — founded by Harvard undergraduates — already gets government funds. Rivers contends that the faith-based initiative is needed for smaller churches that lack such expertise. Small churches ranging from 20 to 300 members account for 95 percent of black church attendance, he says, and "They're closest to the poor."

But skeptics argue that under charitable choice such small churches won't have the resources to deal with the many rules and regulations requiring auditing and accounting that will be imposed in order to ensure that faith-based organizations do not spend federal funds on prohibited activities, like conversion and worship.

---

[1] Ram A. Cnaan and Stephanie C. Boddie, *Black Church Outreach* (2001), University of Pennsylvania, Center for Research on Religion and Urban Society, pp. 1-2.

[2] Ram Cnaan and Gaynor I. Yance, "Our Hidden Safety Net," in E.J. Dionne Jr. and John J. DiIulio Jr., *What's God Got to Do With the American Experiment?* (2000), pp. 154-156.

---

against employers discriminating on the basis of religion. Religious organizations already have an exemption under Title VII of the act permitting them to hire people of their own faith. But the question is whether they should be allowed to discriminate once they take federal funds.

Proponents of the exemption argue that Roman Catholic organizations should be allowed to limit their employees to Catholics, much like Planned Parenthood can decide not to hire someone who is anti-abortion.

"I think it's quite arguable the exemption is constitutionally required," says McConnell of the University of Utah School of Law. "If we allow secular groups to confine their hiring to people who share their beliefs, it's highly questionable to say a group whose beliefs are religious in flavor has any less freedom than they do. If a battered-women's shelter has the right to hire feminists, why shouldn't Teen Challenge have the right to hire Christians?"

Chemerinsky of USC disagrees. "In our history, discrimination against religion, race and gender is something to be fought. The defense the other side gives [that groups should be allowed to hire someone who shares their worldview] concedes there will be more discrimination based on religion. And to me that's a bad thing."

Opponents say extending this exemption to federally funded groups creates a loophole where any federal contractor could discriminate in hiring by calling itself a religious organization. In practice, faith-based groups could use religious discrimination as a pretext for discriminating on other grounds like race, gender and sexual orientation, opponents argue. "If you discriminate on other bases and declare it's religious, then no [legal] case can be made," says Rep. Scott of Virginia.

Opponents have raised the specter of a religious group refusing to hire someone of another race because their religion forbids interracial dating or refusing to hire women if their faith disapproves of men and women mingling. A number of court cases have involved the legality of Christian schools firing unmarried female teachers after they became pregnant. At least two courts have said that the Title VII exemption would allow the schools to dismiss a female teacher for adultery but that a dismissal simply for pregnancy would raise the possibility of illegal sex discrimination. [23]

In the most relevant case that came up before the passage of charitable choice, and which may have been the impetus behind the exemption, a court in 1989 refused to allow the Salvation Army to fire an employee who was a Wiccan (a believer in witchcraft) because her salary was paid substantially with tax money. [24]

A pending suit against a state-funded religious organization in Kentucky could set a precedent for a constitutional challenge to charitable choice, according to the lawyers involved, even though it involves state, not federal funding. Alicia Pedreira was fired from her job as a therapist at the Kentucky Baptist Homes for Children, which contracts with the state to help at-risk youth, after her employees discovered she was a lesbian. A letter firing Pedreira explained that her "homosexual lifestyle is contrary to [the Home's] core values." In April, Pedreira and the ACLU filed a federal lawsuit in U.S. District Court in Louisville accusing the home of religious discrimination. [25]

But constitutional scholar McConnell says he sees no legal basis for the case. "To say a religious grantee can't [discriminate] where a secular grantee can is absurd," he says.

More than three-quarters of Americans surveyed oppose allowing federally funded religious groups to hire only people of the same faith, according to the recent Pew poll. [26] That may reflect Americans' deep suspicion of dogma and a general opposition to a "faith test," suggests Wolfe of Boston College. Yet if the belief by a program's employees in the salvation of souls is what makes the program work, there can't be effective programs without commitments to a specific faith, Wolfe adds. "Just about anything that would work would be unconstitutional," he concludes. ■

BACKGROUND

Fighting Poverty

The fundamental argument of Olasky's *The Tragedy of American Compassion* is that religiously based care historically has been the most effective way of tackling poverty.

"Typically, 100 years ago, if an able-bodied guy came to a homeless shelter, they would hand the guy an ax and say, 'Why don't you chop wood for an hour? 'It allowed people to see if he was willing to work,'" Olasky says approvingly. "For those who didn't have the right values, there was pressure to develop them. Today you have to challenge people that don't have the values of work to develop them rather than enable them to stay at a low level of material help."

But several historians disagree with Olasky's argument that this early model of harsh compassion dating from the Puritans, which "stressed man's sinfulness," was more effective in eliminating poverty than the government programs of the 1960s.

Olasky argues that the poor were better off in 1890, when charity was in private hands, but the consensus view among historians is that the proportion of poor Americans was as high in the 19th century as it has ever been since, according to a critique of Olasky in *The American Prospect*. Journalist Eyal Press writes that Olasky's negative account of the 1960s "is curiously silent about Medicare, Medicaid and the expansion of Social Security, which many scholars credit with all but eliminating poverty among the elderly." [27]

The historical argument illuminates a central ideological divide between liberals, who tend to blame poverty on the structure of the economy, and conservatives, who traditionally blame poverty on the individual's lack of values. It also explains the suspicion of liberal groups that the faith-based initiative is just a pretext, as Jacob S. Hacker wrote in *The New Republic*, to "off-load ever-greater portions of the welfare burden onto faith-based groups," thereby jeopardizing the well-being of people who rely on the welfare state. [28]

Some scholars argue that the division between public and private charity has never been as clear-cut as the liberal-conservative debate would suggest. In his book *When Sacred and Secular Mix*, Stephen V. Monsma reports that the majority of religiously based nonprofits that could be considered "pervasively sectarian" by the Supreme Court's standards — and therefore constitutionally ineligible for taxpayers' funds — do, in fact, receive government funds. [29]

Continued on p. 68

Chronology

1880s-1900s
Salvation Army pioneers religiously based social work, which it dubs "practical religion."

1879-1880
Salvation Army begins missionary work in the United States.

1902
Salvation Army receives its first public money for work with "fallen women."

1940s
Supreme Court declares that the First Amendment erected "a wall of separation" between church and state.

1947
In *Everson v. Board of Education of Ewing Township*, the court allows New Jersey to reimburse parents for bus fare to parochial schools.

1960s
Anti-poverty programs are enacted, but welfare rolls swell. Number of nonprofits grows to 250,000, partly in response to Great Society programs.

1964
President Lyndon B. Johnson declares his intention to create a Great Society "without the wretchedness of poverty."

1964-1965
Congress enacts the Economic Opportunity Act, Medicare, Medicaid and food stamp legislation.

1970s
Landmark Supreme Court decisions reiterate church-state separation.

1971
Lemon v. Kurtzman decision holds that aid to parochial schools must be secular in purpose and effect and must not entangle the government.

1980s
Supreme Court weakens its opposition to public aid to parochial schools.

1985
Supreme Court strikes down two programs providing remedial services to parochial students in *Grand Rapids School District v. Ball* and *Aguilar v. Felton*.

1987
A woman whose salary is paid partially by a federal grant successfully sues the Salvation Army for firing her for practicing the Wiccan religion. The case inspires then-Sen. John Ashcroft, R-Mo., to craft "charitable choice" provisions.

1988
Supreme Court approves federal grants to religiously affiliated charities in *Bowen v. Kendrick*.

1990s
Supreme Court opens door further to public aid to religion. Religious groups push for the right to receive federal funds without giving up their religious identity.

1995
Texas agency threatens to close a branch of Teen Challenge, a Christian drug rehab program, for not using licensed counselors. Gov. George W. Bush exempts faith-based groups in Texas from licensing. Ashcroft introduces "charitable choice" amendment.

1996
President Clinton signs welfare reform bill containing "charitable choice" provisions.

1997
In *Agostini v. Felton* the court upholds aid to parochial schools under the same program it had restricted 12 years earlier.

1998
Clinton signs the Community Services Block Grant bill containing "charitable choice" provisions.

2000s
Newly elected President Bush proposes his faith-based initiative.

June 28, 2000
In *Mitchell v. Helms*, the Supreme Court allows a government-funded computer loan program for parochial schools.

Oct. 17, 2000
Congress reauthorizes law permitting faith-based groups to seek federal aid for drug rehabilitation.

Jan. 29, 2001
President Bush creates Office of Faith-Based Initiatives.

March 28, 2001
Bill introduced to expand charitable choice to nine federal programs.

Continued from p. 66

According to DiIulio, more than a third of the child care in the United States is faith-based, and mothers on welfare have been permitted to use vouchers for child care since 1990. The largest faith-based nonprofit, Lutheran Services in America, receives 39 percent of its $7 billion from government sources. The Salvation Army, which has received government funds since the 1890s, receives 18 percent of its $2.1 billion from government sources. [30]

With the expansion of federal domestic programs, nonprofit groups in general have taken an increasingly important role in social services. In the domestic sector, the federal government funds six private employees for every government employee, according to DiIulio, creating in essence a "government by proxy."

The Salvation Army, according to Lt. Col. Paul Bollwahn, the Army's national social services secretary, has insisted on retaining its Christian identity in its wide array of services for the poor, balking at past demands from a Department of Housing and Urban Development administrator that the Army remove a cross from the wall. While Bollwahn says the Army would not use government-funded programs to evangelize a homeless person, he says, "I wouldn't consider prayers a violation."

Church and State

The country's first political compromise between religious and non-religious factions was embodied in the Constitution's First Amendment, barring the government from establishing a religion. It was a compromise between Enlightenment thinkers like James Madison and Thomas Jefferson, who were suspicious of religion, and Baptists, akin to today's conservative evangelicals, who feared the government establishment of a liberal religion like the Anglican Church.

Today the heirs of Madison and Jefferson can be found in America's civil-liberties groups arguing that the Constitution was intended to prevent all aid to religion, while the Baptists' heirs argue that the First Amendment was intended to prevent the establishment of a state religion. "It meant both things," Boston College's Wolfe says.

Until the 1940s, there was little controversy about the unofficial recognition of religion in America, as evidenced by the widespread practice of prayers in public school. Anti-Catholic feeling, as much as civil-liberty concerns, characterized the predominantly Protestant nation's hostility to the alliance of church and state, according to some accounts. [31] When Catholic immigrants from Ireland began flooding America in the 1840s, Protestants strongly opposed government assistance to Catholic schools.

Supreme Court Rulings

In the late 1940s, a strong trend toward separation emerged, reflected in several historic court decisions. The 1947 *Everson v. Board of Education* ruling set forth the principle that there should be "no aid to religion" even though the case actually permitted parents to be reimbursed for their children's bus transportation to religious schools.

In 1971, in the landmark *Lemon v. Kurtzman* case, the court for the first time struck down a public program that provided money to a religious organization. [32] The court set out a three-part test for permitting assistance to parochial schools: aid had to be secular in purpose, secular in effect and must not entangle the government in its administration.

During the 1970s, the court continued to hand down rulings that further strengthened the wall between church and state. In 1985, the court struck down two other programs that provided remedial services to students in parochial schools in *Grand Rapids School District v. Ball* and *Aguilar v. Felton.*

But the court gradually weakened its restrictions against public aid to church-affiliated schools over the next decade or so, criticizing the *Lemon* test as too rigid in two cases in 1986 and in 1993. In each, the court stressed that the aid went to the individual not the school.

While most court cases have involved funding for religious elementary and secondary schools, the courts have drawn implications for other faith-based institutions providing social services. Only one modern case has focused specifically on social-services groups. In 1988, the Supreme Court approved health and welfare grants to religiously affiliated charities in *Bowen v. Kendrick.* [33] In 1997, in *Agostini v. Felton*, the court moved even further from its earlier separationist stance by upholding aid to parochial schools under the same government program it had restricted 12 years earlier in *Aguilar v. Felton.* Most recently, in *Mitchell v. Helms*, decided on June 28, 2000, the court voted, 6 to 3, to permit a government-funded computer-lending program to parochial schools to continue.

Charitable Choice

From the point of view of Ronald J. Sider, president of Evangelicals for Social Action, the application of the Supreme Court's no-aid policy by the courts has been "confusing," and rulings attempting to separate the secular aspects from religiously based programs have often seemed arbitrary.

"As a result of this legal confusion," Sider wrote last year, "some

Ex-Cop Reels Kids In

While on patrol during his 20-year career as a Washington, D.C., police officer, Tom Lewis often was approached by hungry, neglected children. More than one asked, "Will you be my daddy?" Lewis recalls. He often gave them food, but he was determined to find a better way to help.

"I promised God if I lived long enough to retire, I would do something about it," Lewis recalls. True to his vow, Lewis in 1990 opened the Fishing School in a rowhouse in a run-down neighborhood in northeast Washington.

Lewis had fixed up the building with help from his family and volunteers, and eventually expanded it into the abandoned house next door. Since then he has opened a second school in a nearby neighborhood. The two faith-based, after-school family and child-support centers are staffed by 14 paid employees and volunteers.

The centers' year-round programs serve up to 80 kids a day. Each afternoon staff members pick up the children at their local schools. The children, most of whom are in grades 1-8, typically stay at the Fishing School until 7:30 p.m., participating in activities designed to increase their educational and spiritual capacities.

Children take part in arts and crafts, singing, scripture reading and praying. They also receive computer instruction and learn Spanish. Tutors help with homework and regularly check with their teachers to see if the kids are on target to meet D.C. educational standards.

Parents are vital to the entire process, Lewis says. Sessions are held with parents to discuss the children's progress and offer support. Workshops help parents maintain a healthy family environment. Lewis says he does not want the Fishing School to take the children away from their families, but bring them back. "When programs work, children go back to their parents," he says.

When Lewis found out that many kids who attend the Fishing School don't go home to a cooked meal, he hired a cook, so every child would have a hot meal each evening.

Lewis says the many letters he's received from parents and teachers citing improvement at home and in school convince him that he's on the right track, as do improved report cards and reading and math test scores. Although there are no official statistics, Lewis estimates that about 80 percent of the Fishing School children graduate from high school. And several former Fishing School students have won college scholarships, he says.

The school receives no federal funds but solicits private donations and grants. Whenever he can, Lewis attends what he calls "hope meetings"— events where he tells his story and hopes someone will help. Lewis also hopes that passage of faith-based legislation will help alleviate his 14-hour days by allowing him to hire more trained staff.

There are no restrictions on who can attend the school, but programs do contain Christian-based themes and daily prayer. "If God made you, we'll take you," is his motto.

Lewis says faith-based groups like his are more effective than government services because there's "a sense of loving" at the Fishing School not found in public programs. "There is something that keeps the children here and coming back," he says.

— *Scott Kuzner*

Courtesy Tom Lewis

Former policeman Tom Lewis, back row, center, started the Fishing School to help the neglected children he encountered on his beat. Now he serves 80 kids daily.

---

agencies receiving public funds pray openly with their clients, while other agencies have been banned even from displaying religious symbols." [34]

The issue caught the attention of then-Texas Gov. George W. Bush in 1995, when the Texas Commission on Alcohol and Drug Abuse threatened to shut down a San Antonio branch of Teen Challenge for failing to employ licensed drug counselors. Bush backed the group, granting it an exemption from state regulation and signing a law exempting faith-based groups in Texas from state licensing requirements. [35]

In 1995, then-Sen. Ashcroft introduced the first charitable choice provision — which eventually became part of the 1996 welfare reform bill. In committee, Ashcroft made note of a 1987 court case assessing the Salvation Army $1.3 million in damages for firing an employee from a domestic-violence shelter for her association with the Wiccan religion. Ashcroft feared the case would "send a chill" through religious communities and argued for an amendment guaranteeing religious groups "the ability, frankly to be discriminating" in federal contracts. [36]

The provision was initially adopted as part of the conference agreement with very little notice. No hearings were held on the provision. The bill was signed into law on Aug. 22, 1996.

A charitable choice provision was also approved by Congress in 1998 as part of the Community Services Block Grant Program. In the 106th Congress, Congress enacted two overlapping charitable choice provisions that permitted religious groups to apply for grants to administer substance-abuse prevention and treatment programs. [37] In the Senate floor debate, Ashcroft said the purpose of the amendment was to put churches and other faith-based providers on "an equal footing" with other private organizations in providing federally funded services. He argued that when "people of faith" get involved "the results can be stunningly successful." [38]

The Salvation Army, which was actively involved in drafting the Ashcroft amendment, supported it in order to aid smaller religious groups that often participate in regional efforts like food pantries, according to Bollwahn. In addition, pressure from government contracts to be less religious had produced "antiseptic" programming at the Salvation Army, and a sense that the federal government was both ignoring and disparaging its historic Christian identity, he said.

But opponents observe that the Salvation Army may have had another motivation for supporting the provision exempting faith-based groups from the

bar on religious discrimination in hiring — the wish to avoid future expensive settlements like the one they paid to resolve the suit by the fired Wiccan employee.

The impetus for today's fight over charitable choice stems from a "new fear" that a combination of Supreme Court decisions and cultural trends has "marginalized religion more than is necessary for religious freedom or desirable for the country," writes E.J. Dionne, a senior fellow at the Brookings Institution and *Washington Post* columnist, in introducing essays from both sides. [39] He cites the argument of Yale Law School Professor Stephen Carter that the country seems to have replaced old prejudices based on race and religion with a new prejudice against belief itself.

"The problem is, if you say the state should be neutral between religion and non-religion, you're choosing non-religion," says Boston College's Wolfe. "It looks fair to a non-believer, but it looks like the establishment of atheism to a believer." ∎

CURRENT SITUATION

Legal Challenges?

F ew states have implemented the existing charitable choice provisions, and even fewer have given grants to faith-based organizations. According to the Center for Public Justice, a pro-religion think tank in Annapolis, Md., that supports charitable choice, fewer than 15 states have implemented charitable choice by issuing regulations or otherwise advertising the eligibility of faith-based groups.

Since passage of the 1996 provisions, only 84 religious groups in nine states have received government funds under the new provisions, according to the center. [40] The center primarily blames foot-dragging by state administrators but concedes some faith-based groups have been wary. In Philadelphia only one church — the African-American Cookman United Methodist — has received a grant under charitable choice — for job training.

"There are longstanding suspicions on both sides," says Stephen Lazarus, senior policy associate at the Center for Public Justice.

A legal challenge to the charitable choice laws has yet to be filed. "The reason there hasn't been a challenge to federal law yet is they haven't been implemented in the way the 'far right' wants them to," and thus there are few existing programs with much of a track record to challenge says Mincberg of People for the American Way. Court challenges aren't likely soon since lawyers for the opposition say any challenge would have to be posed against a specific program that has an established pattern of practice of using federal funds to promote religion. The Clinton Justice Department's stated concerns about the provisions' constitutionality and the Clinton administration's reluctance to implement the program have so far put a damper on the willingness of states to carry out the charitable choice provisions, Mincberg and other experts say.

However, lawyers are eyeing four cases challenging state funding for faith-based programs. These include the discrimination suit against Kentucky Baptist Homes; a suit in Texas challenging the constitutionality of funding a welfare-to-work program where the course text was the Bible; and a Wisconsin suit challenging the constitutionality of a faith-based, residential drug-treatment program that involved Bible study, chapel services and admission interviews that probe religious attitudes. [41]

Continued on p. 72

At Issue:

Should the federal government fund faith-based groups as proposed by President Bush?

STEPHEN LAZARUS

SENIOR RESEARCH ASSOCIATE, CENTER FOR PUBLIC JUSTICE

FROM "THE DISCRIMINATION OLYMPICS," APRIL 9, 2001, WWW.CPJUSTICE.ORG

*i*f advocating discrimination against religious groups were an Olympic sport, some opponents of "charitable choice" would be serious medal contenders. Consider, for example, the arguments made by some Washington lobby groups to deny faith-based organizations the right to provide social services as part of publicly funded welfare programs.

Bronze Medal—American Civil Liberties Union: "Government cannot fund the work of faith-based organizations because, under the Constitution, it can't fund religion." Nice try, but when government buys job training or transportation services from religious organizations, it is not buying "religion." It is buying a specific public service, just as it does from "secular" groups. In fact, charitable choice guidelines explicitly state that no public funds can be used for activities such as worship services or discipleship classes.

Silver Medal — People for the American Way: "Government cannot fund the work of faith-based organizations because they might use religion in hiring staff." It is essential to both the integrity and effectiveness of religious organizations that they hire staff committed to their programs. The Civil Rights Act of 1964 guarantees this right to faith-based groups. Charitable choice says they do not have to give it up when they use public funds.

Gold Medal — Baptist Joint Committee: "Government shouldn't fund the work of faith-based organizations, because whatever government funds, it controls." To keep faith-based groups "free" from government, [this argument] denies the right of faith communities to work with government, even if their faith leads them to do so. This is like the overprotective parent who forbids a child from ever going out to play because [his] child might meet the school bully — except that under this scenario, the playground is off limits for all children.

The argument also misses the mark because charitable choice rules now keep government on a pretty tight leash. These new guidelines require government to respect the rights of faith-based organizations to maintain their religious character. The law explicitly states that . . . they no longer have to turn their programs into "religion-free zones" as a condition of receiving public funds.

Instead of giving their blessing to unfair treatment of religious organizations in the public square, these medal winners should adopt a new game plan: Let government welcome all groups as potential teammates in serving the poor, regardless of their religious commitments, and let each group choose for itself whether or not it wants to participate.

AMERICANS UNITED FOR SEPARATION OF CHURCH AND STATE

FROM "THE BUSH FAITH-BASED INITIATIVE: WHY IT'S WRONG," APRIL 2001, WWW.AU.ORG

*u*nder the First Amendment, American citizens are free to decide on their own whether or not to support religious ministries, and the government must stay out of it. Bush's plan turns that time-tested constitutional principle of church-state separation on its ear.

At its core, Bush's plan throws the massive weight of the federal government behind religious groups and religious conversions to solve social problems. While houses of worship have played an important role in this country since its founding, these institutions have thrived on voluntary contributions.

The president's proposal will allow churches to legally discriminate on the basis of religion when hiring, despite receiving public dollars. A Bob Jones-style religious group, for example, could receive tax aid to pay for a social service job, but still be free to hang up a sign that says "Jews And Catholics Need Not Apply."

Under Bush's approach, religious institutions would receive taxpayer support to finance social services and would still be free to proselytize people seeking assistance, seriously threatening the religious freedom of beneficiaries.

Government always regulates what it finances, because public officials are obliged to make certain that taxpayer funds are properly spent. Once churches, temples, mosques and synagogues are financed by the public, some of their freedom will be placed in jeopardy by the almost certain regulation to follow.

Many supporters of Bush's proposal have insisted that faith-based institutions are better, and far more successful, than secular service providers. However, little empirical research supports these claims, and it is unwise to launch a major federal initiative with so little research in the area.

For years, public funds have provided services at religiously affiliated organizations. Catholic Charities and Lutheran Social Services, for example, often have received government grants and contracts. However, strict safeguards have been in place to protect the interests of taxpayers and the religious liberties of those receiving assistance. Independent religious agencies, not churches themselves, handled the public funds. Tax dollars supported only secular programs, and no religious discrimination with public funds was permitted.

Courts found this approach to be consistent with the First Amendment. Bush's plan radically alters that setup by allowing churches and other houses of worship to preach, proselytize and discriminate while providing public services.

Helping Welfare Families in Brooklyn

On Monday mornings, the staff at a storefront Pentecostal Baptist church in Brooklyn hauls the altar to a back room, pushes the chairs against the wall and sets up three offices to help welfare mothers find work.

Judah International Christian Center, an African-American church with about 50 members, is one of 16 religious groups that New York City has hired to help families whose welfare benefits are about to end. The program is the city's first attempt to carry out the so-called charitable choice provisions of the 1996 Welfare Reform Act, which permits religious institutions to receive federal funds for providing social services.

Under the nine-month, $3 million pilot program, which began last September, churches receive several hundred dollars for every person that they help find a job or that they help reconnect with the city's welfare system.

The faith-based groups are successfully reaching clients that didn't respond to letters and phone calls from government agencies and traditional contractors, says Joseph Capobianco, assistant director of the welfare-to-work division at the New York State Department of Labor. "These people are skeptical of government," he says. "The question is: Can organizations with a different relationship, based in the local community and who may know the individuals, do something to help them?"

So far, the churches' intensive door-knocking and phone calling has reached at least 800 individuals, Capobianco says.

In addition, Judah's intimate, one-on-one setting is a far cry from the city's crowded welfare offices, run by the Human Resources Administration (HRA), where mothers with children in tow can wait hours to see a caseworker. Further, many women perceive the jobs the city finds them, such as road clean-up, "degrading," says Keyon Sheppard, Judah's welfare project coordinator.

Judah takes a "holistic" approach to clients, not just finding a job but tackling individual issues, like self-esteem, drug addiction, domestic violence and the need for child care. "Our concern is the total person," Sheppard says. "We ask 'Who is this person?' and [figure out] how to go from where they are to where the HRA would like them to be.

"There's an entire mentality that goes with being a working person as opposed to being at home," he adds. "It's a change of mindset."

Sheppard says the church identifies itself as a faith-based organization when it contacts each welfare recipient, but the program does not discriminate against those of other faiths. "I am a person of faith and that's what makes it faith-based," says Judah's pastor, the Rev. Cheryl G. Anthony. "If a Muslim woman comes in and needs services, we are going to provide services and never question her about her beliefs."

Advocates for the poor question whether the faith-based initiative is an attempt to reduce the federal government's role in helping the poor by shifting the burden to churches.

The Rev. Anthony doesn't think so. "There is a partnership that can happen," Anthony says, "and we need to look at ways to have it happen."

Continued from p. 70

"The fight is about [programs like] Teen Challenge and the program in Wisconsin, where religion is the methodology," says Stern of the American Jewish Congress, which is involved in several of the state challenges.

The Bush Initiative

Most congressional observers expect little controversy over the tax portion of Bush's initiative, which would encourage charitable giving to faith-based organizations by, among other things, permitting taxpayers who do not itemize to deduct their contributions. Sens. Rick Santorum, R-Pa., and Joseph I. Lieberman, D-Conn., introduced such a bill on March 21 to encourage charitable giving through tax incentives.

Most of the controversy is expected to focus on proposals to expand charitable choice to additional federal grant programs. In the House, a bill introduced on March 28 by Reps. J.C. Watts Jr., R-Okla., and Tony P. Hall, D-Ohio, with Bush administration support, incorporates direct aid to faith-based groups as well as the tax incentives. The bill would allow federal funds to flow directly to faith-based groups for nine new programs focusing on juvenile delinquency, crime prevention, housing grants, job training, senior citizens, child care, community development, domestic violence and hunger relief. [42]

Because the faith-based initiative involves so many programs, it is expected to move through multiple committees in many different bills, rather than as one legislative package.

Congressional attention is expected to focus first on Bush's proposal to open competitive bidding to faith-based groups to provide federally funded after-school programs for low-income children.

Bush's proposed budget includes $67 million for both faith-based and secular counseling of prisoners' children, $64 million for programs to promote marriage and help low-income fathers leave welfare, $33 million for group homes to provide shelter for teen mothers and $89 million in a "Compassion Capital Fund" to help start new charities. The Department of Justice budget under Bush's proposal would reallocate $5 million in Federal Bureau of Prisons funds to support faith-based counseling of prisoners about to be released. [43]

Opponents of the Bush initiative have focused much of their discussion on welfare families who will be pushed off the welfare rolls when the five-year federal clock runs out this year. They criticize Bush for opening welfare-to-work and other programs to an increasing number of competing providers without increasing the overall funding available for the disadvantaged.

"Bush is not proposing a bigger pie, he's proposing to divide that pie into a lot more slices. We're very concerned that the net effect will be worse," says Mincberg of People for the American Way. His organization is particularly troubled by Bush's proposal that states provide tax credits for donations to charities and finance it out of the state's share of federal welfare-to-work funds. [44] That's "literally robbing Peter to pay St. Paul."

Bush also has ordered an audit, expected to be completed this summer, to identify barriers to the participation of faith-based groups in federal grant programs administered by five Cabinet agencies. Most expect the investigation will lead to more aggressive implementation of existing laws to include faith-based groups in federal grant programs. ∎

OUTLOOK

Falling Wall?

T his year will mark the first time Congress has held hearings on charitable choice and debated it in the full light of day.

Even if new legislation is passed, the debate will continue, since constitutional challenges in the courts are likely. The challenges are not expected, however, until programs have had time to work at the state and local level. While no Supreme Court ruling is likely anytime soon on charitable choice, constitutional scholars are watching a case challenging Cleveland school vouchers for clues on where the Supreme Court is heading on church vs. state issues.

Any change in the makeup of the Supreme Court during the Bush administration, some conservatives predict, would give a majority to the "neutrality" view shared by four justices that government aid to religion is constitutional as long as it is evenhanded. Currently there is no clear majority opinion on that question. But public-interest groups are already gearing up for the possibility that one of the three justices over age 70 will retire soon, enabling Bush to appoint another conservative.

The shifting and sometimes surprising alignments over the role of faith in America may make some fear that the wall between church and state is tumbling down, columnist Dionne has observed. But he suggests something more complex may be happening as the nation struggles over the appeal and the threat of religiously motivated help to the disadvantaged.

"The turn of the millennium in America may well be remembered as the time when the country renegotiated the relationship between religion and public life, faith and culture." [45] ∎

Notes

[1] See David Nather, "Bush Social Policy Comes Into Focus with Cutbacks, Shift to Local Programs, *CQ Weekly*, April 14, 2001 p. 826.

[2] Under existing law, charitable choice applies to the four following domestic programs: Temporary Assistance to Needy Families (1996), Welfare-to-Work (1997); Community Services Block Grants (1998) and drug treatment under the Substance Abuse and Mental Health Services Administration (2000). For background, see Christopher Conte, "Welfare, Work and the States," *The CQ Researcher*, Dec. 6, 1996, pp. 1057-1080.

[3] David M. Ackerman *et al.*, "CRS Report for Congress: Charitable Choice: Constitutional Issues through the 106th Congress," Dec. 27, 2000, Congressional Research Service.

[4] The Pew Forum on Religion & Public Life and The Pew Research Center for the People & the Press, "Faith-Based Funding Backed, But Church-State Doubts Abound," April 10, 2001, p. 13. (59 percent of Americans oppose allowing groups that encourage religious conversion as part of their social services to compete for federal funds.)

[5] See Pat Robertson, "Mr. Bush's Faith-Based Initiative is Flawed," *The Wall Street Journal*, March 12, 2001.

[6] Labor unions, including the American Federation of State, County and Municipal Employees, joined with progressive religious groups, including the Union of American Hebrew Congregations, in a letter sent to Congress on April 11 urging rejection of Bush's faith-based plan. See Kevin Eckstrom, "Faith-Based Opponents, Supporters Gear up for Capitol Hill Battle," Religion News Service, April 12, 2001.

[7] For background, see Richard L. Worsnop, "Helping the Homeless," *The CQ Researcher*, Jan. 26, 1996, pp. 73-96.

[8] Marvin Olasky, *The Tragedy of American Compassion* (1992), p. 224.

[9] John J. DiIulio, Jr., "Godly People in the Public Square," *The Public Interest*, fall 2000, pp. 113-114.

[10] Byron R. Johnson, *The Role of African-American Churches in Reducing Crime among Black Youth*, University of Pennsylvania, Center for Research on Religion and Urban Civil Society (2001), and Johnson, *A Better Kind of High* (2000).

[11] David Reingold, "Empirical Evidence on Welfare Reform and Faith-Based Organizations," presented at 22nd Annual Research Conference of Association for Public Policy Analysis and Management, Seattle, Wash., November 2000.

[12] See Mark Silk, "Old Alliance, New Ground Rules," *The Washington Post*, Feb. 18, 2001, p. B3.

[13] Mark Chaves, "Congregations' Social Service Activities," Policy Brief No. 6, The Urban Institute, December 1999. at www.urban.org.

[14] DiIulio, op. cit., p. 114.

[15] Christopher Winship and Jenny Berrien, "Boston Cops and Black Churches," The Public Interest, summer 1999, pp. 52-68.

[16] Robertson, op. cit. Also see Gustav Niebuhr, "Promise and Pitfalls Seen in Taking Religion to Prison," The New York Times, April 12, 2001, p. A26. For background, see "Prison-Building Boom," The CQ Researcher, Sept. 17, 1999, pp. 815-838.

[17] Wilson authored The Moral Sense (1993), an examination of the "moral sense" that Wilson argues governs human conduct throughout different periods.

[18] James Q. Wilson, "Religion and Public Life," in E.J. Dionne Jr. and John J. DiIulio Jr., eds., What's God Got to Do With the American Experiment? (2000), pp. 169-170.

[19] Ibid., p. 167.

[20] From James Madison, "Memorial and Remonstrance" (1785) see www.au.org.

[21] Ackerman, op. cit., p. 33.

[22] James Q. Wilson, "Why Not Try Vouchers?" The New York Times, April 27, 2001, p. A25.

[23] The two cases are Vigars v. Valley Christian Center of Dublin, California (1992) and Ganzy v. Allen Christian School (1998).

[24] The case Dodge v. Salvation Army is cited in Dionne, op. cit., p. 141.

[25] Eyal Press, "Faith-Based Furor," The New York Times Magazine, April 1, 2001, p. 62.

[26] Pew, op. cit.

[27] Eyal Press, "Lead Us Not into Temptation," The American Prospect, April 9, 2001.

[28] Jacob S. Hacker, "Faith Healers," The New Republic Online, June 10, 1999. Hacker is a fellow at the New America Foundation.

[29] Stephen V. Monsma, When Sacred and Secular Mix (2000), p. 121. A "pervasively sectarian" organization is a term the Supreme Court has used to refer to "an institution in which religion is so pervasive that a substantial portion of its functions are subsumed in a religious mission." The court has generally barred the flow of tax funds to pervasively religious organizations.

[30] Mark Silk, "Old Alliance, New Ground Rules," The Washington Post, Feb. 18, 2001, p. B3.

[31] Dionne and DiIulio, op cit., p. 117.

[32] Lemon v. Kurtzman.

[33] Bowen v. Kendrick.

[34] Ronald J. Sider and Heidi Rolland Unruh, "No Aid to Religion?" in Dionne and DiIulio, op. cit., p. 129.

[35] Press, op. cit.

[36] See Press, "Faith-Based Furor," op. cit., p. 65.

[37] The two laws, both enacted in 2000, are the Children's Health Act and the Community Renewal Tax Relief Act. See Ackerman, op cit.

[38] Ibid., p. 13.

[39] E.J. Dionne, "The Third Stage," in Dionne and DiIulio, op. cit., p. 119.

[40] Amy Sherman, The Growing Impact of Charitable choice: A Catalogue of New Collaborations Between Government and Faith-Based Organizations in Nine States, Center for Public Justice (March 2000). See "Charitable Choice: Growing Impact," at www.cpjustice.org.

[41] The Texas suit, American Jewish Congress and Texas Civil Rights Project v. Bost, was originally filed in the state courts of Texas and was remanded by the District Court to the state court. The Wisconsin case, Freedom from Religion Foundation v. Thompson, was filed in the federal district court. American Jewish Congress v. Bernik, filed in Superior Court in San Francisco challenges California's state set-aside of $5 million for faith-based programs aimed at helping people re-enter the work force. See Memo from Marc D. Stern, American Jewish Congress "Re: Charitable Choice Litigation," Feb. 23, 2001.

[42] See "Highlights of Faith-Based Initiative Proposals," CQ Weekly, March 24, 2001, p. 661, and David Nather, "House GOP Bets on Passing Aid to 'Faith-Based' Groups; Senate Keys on Tax Incentives." CQ Weekly, March 24, 2001, p. 661.

[43] See David Nather, "Bush Social Policy Comes Into Focus with Cutbacks, Shift to Local Programs," CQ Weekly, April 14, 2001, p. 826.

[44] See David Nather, "Welfare Overhaul's Next Wave," CQ Weekly, March 17, 2001, p. 585.

[45] Dionne and DiIulio, op cit., p. 115.

FOR MORE INFORMATION

Americans United for Separation of Church and State, 518 C St., N.E., Washington, D.C. 20002; (202) 466-3234; www.au.org. This 60,000-member national organization advocates for church-state separation and opposes the faith-based initiative.

Manhattan Institute for Policy Research, 52 Vanderbilt Ave., New York, N.Y. 10017; (212) 599-7000; www.manhattan-institute.org. This research organization's Jeremiah Project, which was originally headed by John J. DiIulio Jr., studies and promotes the work of inner-city ministers in reducing youth violence.

Center for Public Justice, P.O. Box 48368, Washington, D.C. 20002-0368; (410) 571-6300. www.cpjustice.org. This policy research organization, whose stated purpose includes "to serve God," supports government funding for faith-based groups. It posts numerous studies and editorials on its Web site.

Pew Forum on Religion and Public Life, 1150 18th St., N.W., Suite 775, Washington, D.C. 20036-3823; (202) 955-5075; www.pewforum.org. The forum sponsors research and panel discussions on faith-based groups and related polls by the Pew Research Center for the People and the Press.

About the Author

Sarah Glazer, a freelancer in New York who specializes in health and social-policy issues, writes for The Washington Post and other publications. Her recent reports for The CQ Researcher include "Cell Phone Safety" and "Community Prosecution."

Bibliography

Selected Sources Used

Books

Dionne Jr., E. J., and John J. DiIulio Jr., eds., *What's God Got to Do with the American Experiment?* Brookings Institution Press, 2000.

This book of essays, edited by DiIulio, head of the Office of Faith-based and Community Initiatives, and *Washington Post* columnist Dionne, includes arguments for and against government funding of religious groups.

Glenn, Charles L., *The Ambiguous Embrace: Government and Faith-based Schools and Social Agencies*, Princeton University Press, 2000.

A Boston University professor advocates more government support for religious groups, but points out that groups like the Salvation Army have been forced to "secularize" their services to their detriment.

Monsma, Stephen V., *When Sacred and Secular Mix: Religious Nonprofit Organizations and Public Money*, Rowman & Littlefield.

A Pepperdine University professor argues that religious nonprofit organizations play a much larger role in providing social services with public money than one would think.

Olasky, Marvin, *The Tragedy of American Compassion*, Regnery, 1992.

Widely viewed as influential in spurring the Bush administration to fund faith-based groups, the editor of a weekly Christian news magazine argues that religious charities that require work with a handout have historically been more effective than government anti-poverty programs.

Articles

Cole, David, "Faith Succeeds where Prison Fails," *The New York Times*, Jan. 31, 2001.

A self-described "card-carrying liberal" favors public funding for faith-based groups on the grounds that they emphasize treatment rather than incarceration.

Foer, Franklin, and Ryan Lizza, "Holy War: The Faith-Based Slugfest," *The New Republic*, April 2, 2001, pp. 14-17.

The political implications of evangelical Christians' criticism of the faith-based initiative are discussed.

Press, Eyal, "Faith-Based Furor," *The New York Times Magazine*, April 1, 2001, pp. 62-65.

The firing of a lesbian from the Kentucky Baptist Homes for Children has been widely cited by civil libertarians as an illustration of the dangers of permitting faith-based groups to discriminate in hiring.

Press, Eyal, "Lead Us Not Into Temptation," *The American Prospect Online*, April 9, 2001.

The author casts a critical eye on the historical and political arguments for the faith-based initiative and the studies cited supporting the effectiveness of religious groups.

Silk, Mark, "Old Alliance, New Ground Rules," *The Washington Post*, Feb. 18, 2001, p. B3.

Silk, a professor at Trinity College, examines the potential of religious congregations to perform social services and suggests that if they get federal funding they could form a new interest group for the poor.

Szalavitz, Maia, "Why Jesus Is Not a Regulator," *The American Prospect*, April 9, 2001.

The author warns that efforts by the Bush administration to exempt religious groups from state licensing could lead to scandal.

Winship, Christopher, and Jenny Berrien, "Boston Cops and Black Churches," *The Public Interest*, summer 1999, pp. 52-68.

Harvard sociologist Winship praises Boston's black ministers' work with gangs, which has been widely cited by supporters of the faith-based initiative.

Reports

Cnaan, Ram A., "Keeping Faith in the City: How 401 Urban Religious Congregations Serve Their Neediest Neighbors," Center for Research on Religion and Urban Civil Society, University of Pennsylvania.

This report has been widely cited as evidence that urban churches are actively providing social services outside their congregations.

Johnson, Byron, "The Role of African-American Churches in Reducing Crime Among Black Youth, 2001," Center for Research on Religion and Urban Civil Society, University of Pennsylvania.

The center established by John J. DiIulio Jr. finds that churchgoing reduces the likelihood that poor, black youth will be involved in violent crime.

Pew Forum on Religion and Public Life and The Pew Research Center for the People and the Press, "Faith-Based Funding Backed, but Church-State Doubts Abound," April 10, 2001.

Americans think religious groups can do a good job of providing social services but have doubts about how government funding of such groups would work in practice.

Bush Is Said to Scale Back His Religion-Based Initiative

By Elizabeth Becker

WASHINGTON, Oct. 13—President Bush has set aside his most ambitious plans to give federal money to religious charities and instead will support a watered-down version of his religious-based initiative, senators and administration officials say.

Both the pressures of the war on terrorism and the national outpouring of charitable donations since Sept. 11 persuaded the White House to abandon the most contentious parts of the measure to win passage of a law to help charities this year.

"Part of the reason behind the bill was to inspire people to do more, and they have done that," said Senator Rick Santorum, the Pennsylvania Republican and co-sponsor of the president's bill. "While I'm hopeful that what we're seeing in America is real change, we can do more to make this spirit of giving permanent."

The White House said the president hoped to move ahead with the full bill next year, but the religion-based measure could be another victim of the reversal of the presidential priorities since the terrorist attacks on the World Trade Center and the Pentagon.

The House passed a religion-based bill this summer largely along party lines. Democrats were critical of so-called charitable choice provisions that would allow religious groups receiving federal money to hire only members of their faith and to disregard antidiscrimination laws.

There was also concern that money meant for social services would be used by these religious groups to spread their faith.

The legislation was stalled in the Senate where the majority leader, Tom Daschle of South Dakota, said he was unlikely to consider the bill soon because of the charitable choice provisions.

But now White House officials said they were working with the Senate to come up with a bill with a broad base of support that could be passed this year. Officials say they hope that some provisions of charitable choice, like those to aid children of prisoners, could be included.

"It is important to help charitable organizations and both faith-based and community-based groups as soon as we can, given their urgent needs," said Ann Womack, a White Hose spokeswoman. "We're trying to get them help this year."

With the president willing to drop some of these provisions, Mr. Santorum plans to put forward legislation in the next two weeks with his co-sponsor Senator Joseph I. Lieberman, the Connecticut Democrat who has built his career as a centrist with a strong interest in helping religions.

About two weeks ago the White House and the two senators began negotiations to pass a religious charity bill that would largely concentrate on changing the tax code to promote more donations and establishing a compassion fund for religious charities.

The House bill grants up to $13 billion in tax relief by allowing people who do not itemize their taxes to deduct $25 in charitable contributions, allowing noncorporate businesses like family restaurants to receive tax credits for food donations, allowing people over age 70 to make tax-free charitable contributions from their Individual Retirement Accounts and raising the cap for deductible corporate charitable donations to 15 percent by 2010 from 10 percent.

The Senate measure would grant up to $50 billion in tax relief for donations, but Mr. Lieberman said the final provisions were still being negotiated.

From *New York Times*, Oct. 14, 2001. Reprinted with permission.

"I think it is a great step forward and I have given the White House my word that I would not withdraw from our joint pursuit of a larger bill sometime in the future," Mr. Lieberman said.

He also said that the majority leader was "quite receptive" to bringing up the scaled-down version of the bill in the next month.

President Bush campaigned for office saying that financing these religious charities was the cornerstone of this "compassionate conservatism," and once in the White House he declared it his signature social issue.

But his agenda to provide money for religious charities ran into trouble not only in Congress but among religious groups and minorities that feared the issue was a direct assault on the constitutional provisions separating church and state.

Then, John J. DiIulio Jr., the director of the White House office for the religious and community initiative, resigned for health and personal reasons.

Mr. DiIulio's last day at work was Sept. 15, and he has not been replaced.

But he has remained in touch with the White House and said it made sense after Sept. 11 to avoid a battle in the Senate over legislation that was meant to promote good works.

"What this means is that the time for any kind of complicated or contentious debate is not now," Mr. DiIulio said in an interview. "The pieces on which there is the broadest agreement should be moved now. There will be time aplenty to accomplish more later on. That is the spirit of the moment."

U.S.-China Relations: The Scenario

China is poised to become a member of the World Trade Organization (WTO), a membership the country has sought for several years. On October 10, 2000, President Bill Clinton signed into law H.R. 4444, a bill that allows the president to extend permanent, normal trade relations to China. The passage of this bill was considered a precursor to China's entry into the WTO, because it signaled to the rest of the world that the Chinese have made sufficient advances in protecting human rights and have opened up their markets.

The law also establishes an executive branch–congressional commission to review China's record on human rights, labor issues, and environmental issues (see the following article by Lori Nitschke, "After the China Bill: Fresh Start for the Trade Expansion Debate"). Composed of U.S. senators, representatives, and executive branch officials chosen by the president, this commission is expected to report annually to Congress and the president about its findings.

As some of the readings that follow suggest, many citizens, lawmakers, and interest groups are not completely convinced that normalizing trade with China is a good idea. In particular, they fear that China's record of human rights violations, exportation of nuclear and biological weapons, and trafficking in pirated intellectual property (such as computer software, video games, compact discs, and videos) will only worsen under normalized trade relations. In contrast, many others believe that opening trade with China will move that nation more quickly toward democracy.

Participants in the simulation will assume that the Senate Foreign Relations Committee has uncovered new evidence of human rights violations in China. In particular, they have received reports from reputable sources that the practice of harvesting organs from prisoners has increased greatly over the past year. The CBS program *Sixty Minutes* also recently aired a special report on the issue, bringing it into the public spotlight.

Meanwhile, assume that the chairman of the Senate Foreign Relations Committee, Jesse Helms, R-N.C., has reintroduced a bill that imposes trade sanctions on China until it ratifies the International Covenant on Civil and Political Rights (ICCPR—available online at www.unhchr.ch/html/menu3/b/a_ccpr.htm). In 2000, Senator Helms voted against normalizing trade relations with China and made impassioned speeches in opposition to bill H.R. 4444 on the Senate floor. In addition, he proposed an amendment (included in the following documents) that required China to ratify the ICCPR and required that the president certify to Congress that China had made improvements in its human rights practices before granting normalized trade relations (see article that follows by Chuck McCutcheon and Lori Nitschke, "China Trade Bill Remains Intact as Senate Rejects Arms Sanctions"). But the amendment proposed by Helms did not pass. Now China has signed the ICCPR but still has not ratified it. In light of the new human rights violations, assume that Senator Helms has reintroduced his legislation with the hope of imposing trade sanctions on the Chinese until there is evidence of improvements in human rights.

In the simulation, the president is preparing to hold a Rose Garden address to discuss and respond to the recently uncovered human rights violations. Members of the White House communications staff will prepare for the president's address and will try to anticipate the questions posed by members of the press. Members of the White House press corps will familiarize themselves with the issues and prepare thoughtful questions to ask the president and the White House team, not only in the Rose Garden but also at the morning gaggle and afternoon briefing, where they will have a chance to question the press secretary.

AMENDMENT NO. 4125

HELMS (AND WELLSTONE) AMENDMENT NO. 4125—
(Senate—September 07, 2000)

(Ordered to lie on the table.)

Mr. HELMS (for himself and Mr. WELLSTONE) submitted an amendment intended to be proposed by them to the bill, H.R. 4444, supra; as follows:

1   On page 2, line 4, before the end period, insert the following: ";

2   On page 4, before line 1, insert the following:

3   '(c) FINDINGS.—Congress makes the following findings:

4   '(1) The People's Republic of China has not yet ratified the United

5   Nations Covenant on Civil and Political Rights, which it signed in

6   October of 1998.

7   '(2) The 1999 State Department Country Reports on Human Rights

8   Practices found that—

9   '(A) the Government of the People's Republic of China continues

10   to commit widespread and well-documented human rights abuses in vi-

11   olation of internationally accepted norms;

12   '(B) the Government of the People's Republic of China's poor

13   human rights record deteriorated markedly throughout the year, as

14   the Government intensified efforts to suppress dissent;

15   '(C) abuses by Chinese authorities exist, including instances of ex-

16   trajudicial killings, torture and mistreatment of prisoners, forced con-

17   fessions, arbitrary arrests and detentions, lengthy incommunicado de-

18   tentions, and denial of due process;

19   '(D) violence against women exists in the People's Republic of China,

20   including coercive family planning practices such as forced abortion and

21   forced sterilization, prostitution, discrimination against women, trafficking

2

1 in women and children, abuse of children, and discrimination against

2 the disabled and minorities; and

3   '(E) tens of thousands of members of the Falun Gong spiritual

4 movement were detained after the movement was banned in July

5 1999, several leaders of the movement were sentenced to long prison

6 terms in late December, hundreds were sentenced administratively to

7 reeducation through labor, and according to some reports, the

8 Government of the People's Republic of China started confining some

9 Falun Gong adherents to psychiatric hospitals.

10 '(3) The Department of State's 2000 Annual Report on International

11 Religious Freedom states that during 1999 and 2000—

12   '(A) "the Chinese government's respect for religious freedom dete-

13 riorated markedly'";

14   '(B) the Chinese police closed many "underground'" mosques, tem-

15 ples, seminaries, Catholic churches, and Protestant "house churches";

16   '(C) leaders of unauthorized groups are often the targets of ha-

17 rassment, interrogations, detention, and physical abuse in the People's

18 Republic of China;

19   '(D) in some areas, Chinese security authorities used threats,

20 demolition of unregistered property, extortion of "fines", interrogation,

21 detention, and at times physical abuse to harass religious figures and

22 followers; and

23   '(E) the Government of the People's Republic of China continued

24 its "patriotic education" campaign aimed at enforcing compliance with

25 government regulations and either cowing or weeding out monks and

26 nuns who refuse to adopt the Party line and remain sympathetic to the

27 Dalai Lama.

28 '(4) The report of the United States Commission on International

29 Religious Freedom—

30   '(A) found that the Government of the People's Republic of China

31 and the Communist Party of China discriminates, harasses, incarcer-

32 ates, and tortures people on the basis of their religion and beliefs, and

3

1 that Chinese law criminalizes collective religious activity by members

2 of religious groups that are not registered with the State;

3   '(B) noted that the Chinese authorities exercise tight control over

4 Tibetan Buddhist monasteries, select and train important religious

5 figures, and wage an invasive ideological campaign both in religious in-

6 stitutions and among the Tibetan people generally;

7   '(C) documented the tight control exercised over the Uighur

8 Muslims in Xinjiang in northwest China, and cited credible reports of

9 thousands of arbitrary arrests, the widespread use of torture, and ex-

10 trajudicial executions; and

11   '(D) stated that the Commission believes that Congress should not

12 approve permanent normal trade relations treatment for China until

13 China makes substantial improvements with respect to religious free-

14 dom, as measured by certain objective standards.

15   '(5) On March 4, 2000, four days before the President forwarded to

16 Congress legislation to grant permanent normal trade relations treat-

17 ment to the People's Republic of China, the Government of the People's

18 Republic of China arrested four American citizens for practicing Falun

19 Gong in Beijing.

20   On page 4, line 22, beginning with "Prior", strike all through page 5,

21 line 6, and insert the following:

22   Prior to making the determination provided for in subsection (a)(1),

23 the President shall transmit a report to Congress certifying that—

24   '(1) pursuant to the provisions of section 122 of the Uruguay Round

25 Agreements Act (19 U.S.C. 3532), the terms and conditions for the ac-

26 cession of the People's Republic of China to the World Trade

27 Organization are at least equivalent to those agreed between the

28 United States and the People's Republic of China on November 15,

29 1999;

30   '(2) the People's Republic of China has ratified the International

31 Covenant on Civil and Political Rights, and that the Covenant has en-

32 tered into force and effect with respect to the People's Republic of China;

4

1 '(3) the People's Republic of China has begun to dismantle its system

2 of reeducation through labor, which allows officials of the People's

3 Republic of China to sentence thousands of citizens to labor camps

4 each year without judicial review;

5 '(4) the People's Republic of China has opened up Tibet and Xinjiang

6 to regular, unhindered access by United Nations human rights and hu-

7 manitarian agencies;

8 '(5) the People's Republic of China has reviewed the sentences of

9 those people it has incarcerated as counterrevolutionaries under the

10 provisions of a law that was repealed in March 1997 and the People's

11 Republic of China intends to release those people;

12 '(6) the People's Republic of China has agreed to establish a high-

13 level and on-going dialogue with the United States on religious freedom;

14 '(7) the People's Republic of China has agreed to permit unhindered

15 access to religious leaders by the United States Commission on

16 International Religious Freedom and recognized international human

17 rights organizations, including access to religious leaders who are im-

18 prisoned, detained, or under house arrest;

19 '(8) the People's Republic of China has provided a detailed response

20 to inquiries regarding the number of persons who are imprisoned, de-

21 tained, or under house arrest because of religious beliefs or whose

22 whereabouts are not known but who were seen in the custody of offi-

23 cials of the People's Republic of China;

24 '(9) the People's Republic of China intends to release from prison all

25 persons incarcerated because of their religious beliefs;

26 '(10) the People's Republic of China has provided a detailed response

27 to inquiries regarding the number of persons who are imprisoned, de-

28 tained, or under house arrest for reasons of union organizing; and

29 '(11) the People's Republic of China intends to release from prison all

30 persons incarcerated for organizing independent trade unions.

31 On page 5, line 10, strike "section 101(a)" and insert "section 101".

China Today

DAVID MASCI

Last October, the People's Republic of China threw itself a party the likes of which hadn't been seen in Beijing in years.

The mammoth event featured a five-mile-long parade that snaked past President Jiang Zemin and other government leaders gathered in Tiananmen Square to celebrate the PRC's 50th anniversary. Some 90 floats depicted the communist state's recent achievements, from its growing industrial might and improved standard of living to its victories in the Olympics.

But the parade also was intended to showcase China as an up-and-coming military power, a point dramatically made by the more than 10,000 white-gloved soldiers and 400 tanks and other military vehicles. (*See sidebar, p. 90.*)

The display of military might was calculated, says James R. Lilley, a resident fellow at the American Enterprise Institute. "They want us to know that they're not going to be pushed around," he says. "Their intention is clear: neutralize American power in the region and press their territorial claims."

Pressing territorial claims has been a priority for China in recent years. On June 30, 1997, the British followed the dictates of a 19th-century treaty and returned Hong Kong to the PRC. Two and half years later, China took back the island of Macao from another former colonial power, Portugal.

But one major prize remains: Taiwan. Unlike Hong Kong and Macao, the island is a de facto independent state, run by a democratically elected government. Bigger than the state of

From *The CQ Researcher,*
August 4, 2000.

More than 500,000 soldiers and civilians took part in a massive parade in Beijing's Tiananmen Square last Oct. 1 celebrating the 50th anniversary of the People's Republic of China.

Maryland, modern Taiwan was founded in 1949 by China's former leader, Chiang Kai-shek, and his Nationalist Party. Chiang and the Nationalists — losers in the civil war that brought the Communists to power — set up a parallel state and proclaimed themselves the legitimate government of all of China.

Until the 1970s, the United States accepted Taiwan as the sole representative of China. But President Richard M. Nixon's groundbreaking visit to the mainland in 1972 set in motion a shift in American policy. Today, the United States recognizes the Communists on the mainland as the legitimate government of China. It also adheres to what is known as the "one China" policy, which maintains that Taiwan should reunite with the mainland, though by peaceful means. [1]

Some experts contend that the "one China" policy is misguided and should be discarded in favor of one that respects the wishes of Taiwan's 26 million people. "Unlike [mainland] China, Taiwan is a democracy, and we need to respect and back up whatever decision [it] makes," says Gary Schmitt, executive director of the Project for the New American Century, a Washington, D.C., think tank that promotes

American global leadership. That includes the right to be independent, he says. [2]

Schmitt and others argue that instead of pushing Taiwan into the arms of the PRC, the United States should be telling the government on the mainland that it will defend the island's right to decide its own fate.

But others say that such a move would be terribly irresponsible and not in America's interests. "Our relationship with China is one of the cornerstones of U.S. foreign policy, and siding squarely with Taiwan would destabilize that relationship and the whole region," says Richard Haass, director of foreign policy studies at the Brookings Institution.

"One China" is a viable strategy, according to Haass, because it "allows Taiwan to continue in its present state without antagonizing the Chinese."

Haass and others also argue that mainland China is becoming a more open society, making the prospect of reunification at some point in the future much more appealing to Taiwan. "Economic changes have already transformed China for the better and will continue to do so," Haass says.

Indeed, those who believe that China is becoming a more open society contend its expected entry into the World Trade Organization (WTO) next year should accelerate the process of liberalization. [3]

"Membership will ultimately make China a more transparent society, one that is more accountable to its people," says David Shambaugh, director of the China Policy Program at George Washington University.

The WTO is a multinational coalition that works to lower barriers to international trade. Supporters of China's entry into the organization argue that increased trade will spur economic growth, creating a middle class that will come to expect greater personal liberty and political freedom.* In addition, supporters say, WTO membership will integrate China further into the world community, pushing the country to adopt international standards, like respect for the rule of law and human rights.

But Margaret Huang, program director for Asia at the Robert F. Kennedy Memorial Center for Human Rights, argues that WTO membership actually may make the Chinese Communists more, not less, repressive. According to Huang, as freer trade forces the government to cede control over the economic sphere, it may feel the need to tighten its hold over political activity. "They may feel more threatened and crack down," she says.

As events in China unfold, here are some of the questions experts are asking:

Should the United States continue to support the "one China" policy?

For the mainland, the meaning of "one China" is simple: Taiwan is a renegade province that must eventually return to the fold. In fact, for most of its 50-year existence, the government in Taipei also envisioned full reunification, though with a Nationalist government at the helm.

But Taiwan now views the "one China" concept more ambiguously. Chen Shui-bian, the island's recently elected president, has said "one China" could have a range of meanings, presumably from some sort of

loose association to complete reunification. But Chen, the first non-Nationalist to hold Taiwan's presidency, has not publicly stated his own definition of the term. [4]

Until recently, there was a lot of ambiguity in how the United States publicly viewed the relationship between Taiwan and China. In 1972, the year Nixon made his trip to China, the United States stated that it "acknowledges that all Chinese on either side of the Taiwan Strait maintain there is but one China and that Taiwan is part of China." [5] In other words, America simply affirmed the view held by both sides without saying anything more.

Even in 1979, when the United States officially shifted diplomatic recognition from Taipei to Beijing, the meaning of "one China" remained nebulous.

But in 1998, President Clinton peeled away some of the ambiguity. While on a visit to Shanghai, the mainland's largest city, he asserted what became known as the "three no's," rejecting the idea of Taiwanese independence, two Chinas or membership for the island in any international organizations that require statehood. [6]

"This was a big mistake for the Clinton administration because we put our cards on the table, we picked a side," says Stephen Yates, a senior policy analyst at the Heritage Foundation, a conservative think tank. "When you say 'one China' and spell out what that means the way Clinton did, you're implying that you want reunification as an outcome and are basically accepting Beijing's argument."

Instead, Yates says, the United States should drop the "one China" policy and simply push for a peaceful resolution of the situation. "This should be about process, not outcome," he argues.

Others favor more openly siding with Taiwan. "Supporting the 'one China' policy is living in the past be-

cause the situation has changed so dramatically since that policy was developed," says Schmitt of the Project for the New American Century. "Taiwan is now a democracy and, frankly, I don't think [its] heart is in this," he says, referring to the prospect of reunifying with the mainland.

Schmitt says the United States needs to "break out" of its current policy and fully back and defend, with military force if necessary, Taiwan's right to self-determination. "We need to make it clear that it's unacceptable for Beijing to do anything to force Taipei into accepting something [it doesn't] want," he says.

But other China experts think that jettisoning "one China" is foolhardy and dangerous. "One China" is the only policy that will bring any resolution to this problem," says George Washington University's Shambaugh. "An independent Taiwan has no future."

Supporters of "one China" contend that if the United States were to publicly abandon the policy, Taiwan's security would be seriously compromised, even with American support. "Taiwan's long-term security cannot be achieved just through weapons but must come through some sort of accommodation with the People's Republic of China," says David M. Lampton, director of China Studies at the School for Advanced International Studies (SAIS) at Johns Hopkins University.

According to Lampton, mainland China's vast population advantage over Taiwan (1.3 billion people vs. 23 million) and close proximity to the island mean that it will be a serious threat to Taiwan as long as it wants to be. And, Lampton, says, China is unlikely to relinquish its claim to the island anytime soon.

"If China went democratic tomorrow," he says, "[it'd] be as tough on Taiwan as [it is] today because this is a great nationalist issue."

Finally, supporters say, "one China" is the best policy for the United States

Inside the World's Most Populous Nation

Former Chinese leader Mao Zedong once likened his vast nation to "another United Nations." The world's most populous country dwarfs tiny Taiwan, off the southeast coast. China has 31 provinces and two special administrative regions, the islands of Hong Kong and Macao. The largest province is Xinjiang, about three times the size of Spain. The most populous province, Sichuan, has more than 110 million residents, about the same as Japan. China's largest city, Shanghai, has 11 million people. Many provinces, including Guangdong, Hubei, Shandong, Jiangsu and Hunan, all have 50-100 million people, similar to such countries as France and Mexico.

While China is more than 90 percent Han Chinese, each region does have its own cultural and economic flavor. Guangdong, in the south, is known for its freewheeling ways and burgeoning economy. Shanghai is China's cultural and financial center. A number of provinces, like Tibet and Xinjiang, have large pockets of non-Chinese ethnic groups and have been designated as "autonomous regions." Nonetheless, separatist movements are active in both provinces.

While China's 1.3 billion people make up more than one-fifth of the world's population, they only occupy one-fifteenth of the Earth's land. And, since much of the Western part of the country is sparsely inhabited, due to the harsh terrain and climate, more than two-thirds of China's people are crowded into the more prosperous eastern part of the country.

China's Golden Coast

GDP per capita, 1998
- $250-500
- $500-750
- $750-1,000
- $1,000+

Source: China Statistical Yearbook

500 km

HEILONGJIANG, JILIN, LIAONING, Beijing, INNER MONGOLIA, XINJIANG, GANSU, HEBEI, Tianjin, SHANXI, NINGXIA, SHANDONG, QINGHAI, SHAANXI, HENAN, JIANGSU, Chongqing, ANHUI, Shanghai, HUBEI, ZHEJIANG, TIBET, SICHUAN, JIANGXI, HUNAN, FUJIAN, GUIZHOU, TAIWAN, YUNNAN, GUANGXI, GUANGDONG, HONG KONG, MACAO, HAINAN

Sources: China Statistical Yearbook, The Economist

because U.S. relations with the mainland are much more important than those with Taiwan. "If we changed this policy, we would cause a serious and fundamental crisis with China," says Nancy Bernkopf Tucker, a professor of history at Georgetown University. "Doing so with such a huge and important country cannot be in the national interest."

Will membership in the World Trade Organization lead to a more open society in China?

Sometime next year, the People's Republic of China will almost certainly join the WTO. Admission will be a major victory for China's Communist government, which spent the last 13 years negotiating terms of entry with the United States and other Western countries.

The WTO is a 135-nation trading club whose members agree to reduce barriers to international commerce. In its bid for membership, China has agreed to significantly lower tariffs on industrial and agricultural goods and reduce existing restrictions on foreign investment.

Supporters of China's application say it will accelerate the country's efforts to develop a modern market economy. U.S. Trade Representative Charlene Barshefsky and other WTO boosters also argue that entry will help China become a more open society. WTO membership will help make China "freer, more open to the world and [more] responsive to the rule of law than it is today," Barshefsky said in May.[7]

"When you inject the seed of capitalism in a place, it naturally breeds openness everywhere," says William

Morley, chief lobbyist for the U.S. Chamber of Commerce, which supports WTO membership for China. Once you give the people economic freedom, they'll begin to want more personal freedom."

Morley predicts that WTO membership will help create a solid middle class that will quickly develop a sense of its rights. "Once people begin enjoying the fruits of their labors," he says, "they inevitably start to demand a greater say in other areas, like politics." And that, adds the Heritage Foundation's Yates, "expands the amount of pressure on the government to become more open and democratic, and to guarantee personal freedom."

Supporters also argue that WTO membership will force China to begin to respect the rule of law, a human rights linchpin in any society. "[WTO membership] will get them much more involved in rules-based behavior," says Johns Hopkins' Lampton, "because without it they won't be able to operate in the international arena."

First, Lampton argues, China will have to develop a more reliable court system to deal with business-related issues such as commercial transactions and intellectual property. But eventually, he says, the openness and reliability will spill over into other areas. "Once you develop a core of people who rely on due process in one realm, they begin to expect it in others," he says.

Finally, WTO supporters contend, freer trade will bring an influx of new ideas and information, via the Internet and a host of other mediums. "This will bring greater access to informa-

tion, especially information from the West," Morley says. "They will become accustomed to the Western way of doing things, and this will have a profound impact on them."

How profound? No one knows, of course. But according to the American Enterprise Institute's Lilley, the influx of new ideas and information from the outside "could very well help to undermine the current system."

House Minority Whip David Bonior, D-Mich., cautions that accession to the WTO may not ultimately

Chinese farmers till the soil on the outskirts of Beijng. Despite China's aggressive push toward modernization and manufacturing, more than two-thirds of its 1.3 billion people still live in rural areas.

be a positive force for change. "Contrary to the assertions of WTO cheerleaders, the hidden hand of the marketplace will not automatically bring about democratic reforms or social progress," Bonior wrote recently. He argues that it was organized protest, not the marketplace, that won Americans greater labor and other rights in the 20th century. [8]

Indeed, some experts say entry into the WTO might shrink political freedoms. "I think things are going to get worse because the government will tighten political control as it loses

more and more authority in the economic sphere," says the Robert F. Kennedy Center's Huang. "There will be more arrests, more crackdowns, more harassment of labor organizers and human rights workers."

Huang predicts additional curtailment of rights and liberties as the opening of the economy leads to massive worker dislocation and other social tensions. "WTO [membership] will lead to millions being laid off as they privatize state-run industries," she says. "The sudden presence of all of these unemployed workers and other changes are going to lead to social upheaval, which will force the government to crack down even more" (*see p. 90*).

And some argue that China will probably try to segregate the system used for international business from the rest of the country's legal infrastructure. "They may well be able to guarantee that commercial law reaches certain standards without changing the way, say, human and labor rights are handled," says Mike Jendrzejczyk, Asia director for Human Rights Watch, an advocacy group that favors China's admittance to the WTO. "My guess is that they'll try." ∎

BACKGROUND

East Meets West

Until relatively recently, China took little interest in the outside world.

Chronology

Secure in its venerable culture and society, the so-called Middle Kingdom usually ignored the world beyond its borders.

Even when the Chinese did venture out, their actions would have seemed alien to Western explorers, conquistadors and adventurers. In the early 15th century, for example, Adm. Cheng He took Chinese naval expeditions as far as East Africa. Cheng was not seeking new lands to conquer or even plunder, however. His mission was "to make 'the whole world' into voluntary admirers of the one and only center of civilization." [9]

But China could not remain closed to the outside world forever, and when European powers took an interest in it in the 19th century, the nation was wholly unprepared.

The first major opening came in 1840, when a British fleet arrived in southern China to force the repeal of measures that had outlawed the lucrative, British-controlled opium trade. Outgunned by the English on sea and land, the Chinese swallowed a peace treaty that not only permitted the opium trade but also ceded Hong Kong to the British and opened five ports to foreigners.

The rest of the 19th century was equally difficult for China. Forays by France, Russia and Japan, in addition to Britain, were common. The foreign meddling, coupled with internal strife, weakened the state tremendously.

In 1911, China's last imperial dynasty, the Qing, fell, and a republic was proclaimed under Sun Yat-sen, a Western-educated reformer. But Sun's republic quickly disintegrated into chaos as independent warlords fought for control of the country.

After World War I, Sun's Nationalist Party, known as the Kuomintang, began working to reunite China. Under Sun's successor, Chiang Kai-shek, and aided by the growing Communist Party, the Nationalists began

1900-1939
China's last imperial dynasty topples.

1911
The last Qing emperor abdicates, and Nationalist Party leader Sun Yat-sen becomes president of the new Republic of China.

1927
Civil war begins between the Communists and Nationalists.

1934
The defeated Communists go on "The Long March" into northern China.

———— • ————

1940-1974
The Communists defeat the Nationalists for control of China.

Oct. 1, 1949
The Communists proclaim the People's Republic of China. Chiang and the Nationalists escape to Taiwan.

1960
Mao taps Deng Xiaoping and other pragmatists to reverse the economic damage caused by an experiment in socialism.

1966
Mao launches "The Cultural Revolution" to eliminate Western influence, killing millions.

1972
President Richard M. Nixon visits China; the U.S. recognizes the Communist government.

1975-Present
Mao is replaced by reformers Deng and Jiang.

1976
Mao dies. Deng launches economic reforms.

1979
President Jimmy Carter resumes full diplomatic relations with the People's Republic and breaks ties with Taiwan.

1989
Pro-democracy protests in Tiananmen Square in Beijing are brutally suppressed by Deng. Jiang Zemin becomes Deng's handpicked successor.

1996
China fires practice missiles near Taiwan; the U.S. dispatches two aircraft carriers to the area.

February 1997
Deng dies; Jiang takes over.

June 30, 1997
Britain returns Hong Kong to China.

Dec. 20, 1999
Portugal returns Macao.

February 2000
China threatens to use military force against Taiwan if the island indefinitely delays reunification talks.

May 2000
Chen Shui-bian becomes president of Taiwan and accepts the "one China" policy.

creating a unified Chinese state.

In 1927, Chiang broke with his Communist allies. Although the Nationalists controlled most of the country, the Communists established a substantial military and even administrative presence in parts of China.

Japanese aggression in Manchuria beginning in 1931 distracted the Nationalists. But in 1934, Chiang refocused his attention on the Communists, routing them in most areas under their control. The scattered Communist army retreated for nearly two years, fighting its way through western China to Shaanxi Province in summer 1936. Known as "The Long March," the odyssey established Mao Zedong as the leader of the Communists. [10]

In 1937, Japanese aggression turned into a full-scale invasion of northern and eastern China, prompting the Nationalists and Communists to bury their differences and confront the Japanese together. But Japan's modern military quickly occupied much of the country.

Chairman Mao

After World War II, Chiang and Mao began fighting again. This time, the Communists were stronger. Mao's genius for organizing had enabled the party and its military wing, now called the People's Liberation Army (PLA), to grow tremendously during the war years. [11]

Chiang's undisciplined army was no match for the well-organized PLA, and by 1949 the Nationalists were in severe trouble. On Oct. 1, the Communists formally established the People's Republic of China, and Chiang and about 200,000 followers fled to Taiwan.

During the first decade of his rule, Mao turned China into a socialist state. Agriculture was collectivized and industry was nationalized. China's first five-year plan, in 1953, set out to develop heavy industry, using the Soviet Union as a model. At the same time, Chinese society became more structured and, for many, more inhospitable. For example, peasants and workers were organized into brigades, while many artists, professionals and businessmen were persecuted as enemies of the party. In 1958, the transformation was accelerated in what came to be known as "The Great Leap Forward," which lasted for two years.

Throughout the first decade of Communist rule, China maintained close relations with the Soviets. China's entry into the Korean War against the United States in 1950 strengthened the tie. But as the 1950s came to a close, Sino-Soviet relations grew colder because of ideological differences and territorial disputes. The freeze would last for three decades.

By 1960, Mao and other Chinese leaders recognized that the Great Leap had been a failure. The economy was in a state of crisis. In response, a new group of pragmatic leaders arose, including Deng Xiaoping. They improved the economy by allowing farm and factory managers more control over production. At the same time, Deng strengthened the Communist Party. [12]

Mao, sensing he was being edged from power, began a campaign against what he said were China's increasingly "capitalist" tendencies. During the so-called Cultural Revolution (1966-1976), Mao purged his political opponents, including Deng. Millions of people were killed, including many of China's leading thinkers, politicians and professionals. Many other educated people were sent to remote parts of China to be "re-educated" through manual labor.

Secure once again, Mao, during his remaining years eschewed the bold — and often disastrous — steps that characterized the first 20 years of his rule. A major exception was the building of better relations with the United States, fostered by President Nixon's historic 1972 trip to China. At the time, each country saw the other as a valuable ally against the Soviet Union.

Deng Takes Over

By the time Mao died in 1976, Deng had been rehabilitated. Mao's trusted lieutenant, Premier Zhou Enlai — himself a pragmatic modernizer — had brought Deng back in 1973 to once again help restructure Chinese society.

But Zhou had died eight months before Mao, leaving a huge leadership vacuum. After a relatively brief struggle for power with Mao's widow and her key supporters (known as the Gang of Four), Deng became paramount leader.

Deng quickly launched a series of ambitious reforms. Collective agriculture was scrapped in favor of the old system of family-run farms. Private enterprise, once illegal, was encouraged, leading to the rapid creation of a new business class. China's market was opened to foreign trade and investment.

Important non-economic changes also were undertaken. Couples were restricted to one child to reduce China's huge population, and diplomatic relations were established with the United States and other Western countries.

In the political arena, though, there was a marked absence of change. The Communist Party retained control of the government and restricted citizens' liberty. The limits on freedom of speech and assembly were dramatically revealed to the world in 1989, when tens of thousands of democracy supporters gathered in Beijing's Tiananmen Square to demand change. After vacillating for a number

China Beefs Up Its Military

For the United States, the 1991 war against Iraq vindicated more than a decade of spending on high-tech armaments. Equipped with so-called smart bombs, Patriot surface-to-air missiles and powerful M-I Abrams tanks, American forces led by Gen. Norman Schwartzkopf dispatched Saddam Hussein's military in a matter of days.

But for China's political and military leadership, the conflict over Saddam's invasion of Kuwait was a wake-up call, many defense experts say. "They were very impressed with U.S. power and realized that their military was decades behind ours," says Harvey Feldman, a senior fellow at the Heritage Foundation's Asia Studies Center.

Since then, the Chinese have been trying to catch up, embarking on a massive effort to buy and develop new weapons and professionalize their military. "They clearly want to be able to challenge U.S. power in the Pacific," says James R. Lilley, a resident fellow at the American Enterprise Institute.

Throughout the 1990s, China's military budget has steadily increased, usually growing by 10 percent or more each year. [1] At the same time, President Jiang Zemin ordered the military to divest its substantial business holdings, which at one point comprised an estimated 20,000 companies employing 16 million people. Profits from these businesses — which included hotels, farms and factories — were used for military purposes. But Jiang worried that China's generals were becoming more concerned with the bottom line than combat readiness.

In some military areas, the Chinese have made substantial progress in recent years. For example, they have developed intercontinental ballistic missiles capable of hitting the West Coast of the United States, as well as other possible adversaries such as Russia, India and Japan. "By next year, they should be able to hit any target in our country," Feldman says.

In addition, the Chinese have made strides in efforts to miniaturize nuclear weapons — aided by stolen U.S. technology, American officials charge. "This allows them to put more than one [nuclear] warhead on their long-range missiles," Feldman says.

In most military areas though, China still lags far behind the United States. For instance, while the 3-million-strong People's Liberation Army is the world's biggest fighting force, many of its troops still use weapons from the 1960s and '70s. And training and tactics are also still antiquated. The navy, and to some extent the air force, fare little better by comparison. "They're still completely out of our league," Feldman says. "In an all-out engagement, we would destroy them."

The Chinese are trying to close the gap by buying sophisticated weapons from abroad, especially from the Russians. They already have purchased two Russian *Sovremenny*-class destroyers with the Sunburn anti-ship missile, one of the most effective weapons of its kind. "This is a particularly bad development, because these missiles can threaten our [aircraft] carriers," Lilley says. "They are difficult if not impossible to defend against," says Michael Pillsbury, a Department of Defense consultant on the Chinese military.

In addition, Beijing has bought a number of Russian fighter planes, including the SU-27 and the more advanced SU-30MK. While these aircraft are a substantial improvement over the rest of China's aging air force, they cannot effectively stand up to F-16, F-18 and other front-line American fighter planes, many experts say.

Actually, the Chinese do not expect these and other weapons purchases to put them on a military par with the United States any time soon, Feldman says. Instead, he says, the Chinese just want to be powerful enough to deter the U.S. from intervening if China were to attack Taiwan, which it has threatened to do if the island declares independence.

"Their short-term goal is to be able to hold us off long enough to destroy the military and economic capability of Taiwan," he says. "And you know, I think they're getting there."

---

[1] Figures cited in Frank Gibney Jr., "Birth of a Superpower," *Time*, June 6, 1999.

---

of weeks, the government violently crushed the protest, killing thousands, according to some reports. [13]

Tiananmen tarnished the regime's image abroad and at home but had little impact on China's reforms or its rapidly growing economy. By the time Deng died in 1997, China had been transformed from an isolated country with an inefficient state-run economy into an economic powerhouse that many say will be a superpower in the next century. [14]

But Deng's passing also left political uncertainties, including whether party elite would accept his handpicked successor, Jiang Zemin.

Unlike Mao and Deng, Jiang was not a founding member of the Communist Party. Moreover, he had not served in the military and consequently lacked strong support within the all-powerful PLA.

Still, Jiang has established a relatively strong power base, placing people loyal to him in important government posts. The smooth takeover of Hong Kong and Macao under Jiang's watch, coupled with China's continued economic growth during the Asian financial crisis, also helped ease uncertainties about his leadership. ■

CURRENT SITUATION

Economic Growth

During the early 1990s, China's economy defied gravity. In 1992, for instance, the gross domestic product (GDP) rose a phenomenal 14 percent. Average growth for the decade was an impressive 10 percent. [15]

Deng's market-opening reforms had brought a vibrant and brash form of capitalism to China, transforming the lives of hundreds of millions.

But economic gravity is a powerful force, and in the second half of the 1990s it returned, although not with enough force to stall the economy. From 1995 to 1999, GDP growth steadily slowed, from 10 percent to 7 percent. [16] During this time, however, most developing economies in East Asia were spiraling into a deep recession.

Still, government spending has fueled much of the growth over the last three years, which in turn has driven up China's budget deficit. "They can't keep pumping up the economy with government stimulus," says Nicholas Lardy, a senior fellow at the Brookings Institution and an authority on China's economy. "What they're doing is ultimately unsustainable," he says, noting that 50 percent of government spending now goes to debt repayment.

Growth also has been sustained by overproduction, experts say. Between 1990 and 1998, an estimated 40 percent of the increase in GDP

was due to the production of products that were not needed and not sold. "They've built up huge inventories that just go into warehouses," Lardy says. "Last year they produced 30 million televisions and sold 20 million, leaving the remaining 10 million in inventory."

Economic Problems

Moreover, the economy still needs more structural reform. Beijing continues to have a huge presence in many commercial areas, a vestige of once-pervasive communism. Most economists believe the government controls between one-quarter and half of the means of production, making everything from telecommunications equipment to autos.

Economists generally agree that a large share of the state-owned businesses are inefficient holdovers, often employing too many workers making products not up to market standards. "Many of them are just not competitive and are losing a lot of money," says Gary Jefferson, a professor of economics at Brandeis University in Waltham, Mass.

Under premier and economic czar Zhu Rongji, the government has been steadily selling off state-owned businesses. "They've made real progress in shrinking the state's presence in the economy," Jefferson says.

Lardy agrees but feels that Rongji has not moved fast enough, out of the legitimate fear that accelerated privatization will put millions of Chinese out of work and could lead to social upheaval. "They clearly need to speed up the pace here because it's such a terribly inefficient use of resources," he says.

The inefficient state sector is also creating another problem. "Because many of these state enterprises are in

financial difficulty, they are putting an enormous strain on the banking system," Jefferson says. Indeed, an estimated 75 percent of the loans made by China's four biggest state banks go to government enterprises. [17] Many of these loans will never be repaid, as both the bankers and company managers well know, Jefferson says. But lending continues because the banks are directed by the government not to let these money-losing firms slide into bankruptcy, he says.

The banking problem is already enormous, Lardy says. As of last year, up to 40 percent of the banking system's $1 trillion in outstanding loans were deemed unrecoverable, largely because of lending to the state sector. [18] "Unless something is done to change this," he says, "the financial system may collapse."

Still, Jefferson sees the overall economic picture as positive. "If international growth rates continue, I predict that China will continue to grow in a stable way," he says, citing healthy exports and continued high levels of foreign investment.

In addition, Jefferson says, China's imminent WTO membership will open the country's markets to more competition, forcing the government to "further accelerate efforts to reduce state participation in the economy. They'll have to move forward rapidly with this if they want to compete." ■

OUTLOOK

Political Change?

In May, President Jiang announced the latest in a long line of efforts to rejuvenate the Chinese Communist

Continued on p. 93

At Issue:

Should Congress link passage of permanent normal trade relations (PNTR) with China to guarantees on human rights reforms?

MIKE JENDRZEJCZYK
Washington director, Asia Division,
Human Rights Watch

FROM TESTIMONY BEFORE THE HOUSE COMMITTEE ON INTERNATIONAL RELATIONS, MAY 10, 2000

china has lobbied for several years for an end to the annual review of its trade status under the Jackson-Vanik amendment of the Trade Act of 1974, and as part of the World Trade Organization (WTO) deal President Clinton has pledged to give China permanent normal trade relations status. . . .

Congress should set concrete, meaningful and realistic human rights conditions that China must meet before receiving PNTR. The president should be required to certify that these conditions have been met, and this could happen any time following China's accession to the WTO.

For example, China should be required to:
• Ratify the two United Nations human rights treaties it has signed: the International Covenant on Civil and Political Rights . . . and the International Covenant on Economic, Social and Cultural Rights;
• Take steps to begin dismantling the huge system of "re-education through labor," which allows officials to sentence thousands of citizens to labor camps each year for up to three years without judicial review;
• Open up Tibet and Xinjiang to regular, unhindered access by U.N. human rights and humanitarian agencies, foreign journalists and independent monitors. . . .

Getting China to meet these conditions is possible, if the administration engages in the kind of intensive, high-level negotiations with Beijing it conducted to finalize the trade agreement last November. In light of the failure of the U.N. in Geneva to censure China, it is even more imperative that Congress and the administration agree on meaningful human rights conditions on PNTR as one of the few remaining sources of serious leverage.

To replace the annual trade-status review, we would strongly support creation of a new mechanism, such as a special commission appointed jointly by Congress and the executive branch along the lines of what Rep. [Sander M.] Levin, [D-Mich.,] has proposed. This commission should issue a report annually on China's compliances with international human rights and labor rights norms.

But this should be more than a pro forma process, or it will have no real credibility. Legislation establishing the commission should require a vote by Congress on the commission's findings and recommendations for U.S. bilateral and multilateral policy initiatives. . . .

WILLARD WORKMAN
Vice president for International Affairs,
U.S. Chamber of Commerce

WRITTEN FOR *THE CQ RESEARCHER*, JULY 2000

using trade as a weapon does more than hurt the working people, farmers and business of the United States — it reduces our economic and social influence abroad. We don't just export goods, we export American ideals.

Throughout the United States and around the world, individual liberty and free enterprise go hand in hand. By their very presence and operations, American companies and the expatriate communities that depend on them contribute mightily to economic, political and religious freedom in their host countries. Continuing U.S. company presence abroad is critical to the inculcation of American civic values.

The U.S. business presence in China has resulted in greater job choice for workers, higher wages and living standards, better workplace safety and health standards, improved education and training opportunities and a host of other benefits sought by workers in the United States, China and all over the world. And as hundreds of millions of Chinese people continue to migrate from the interior to the coastal regions to take advantage of these imported economic opportunities, the potential for expanded U.S. economic, social and cultural influence will be historic.

These workers will make more money, read more Western books and periodicals and receive greater exposure to Western ideals of social, economic and political reform than their compatriots who remain isolated. Unilateral restrictions on U.S. firms in China not only imperil U.S. competitiveness in that country but also compromise a principal source of human progress for nearly one-fourth of the world's people.

No moral person can countenance the atrocities that are committed around the world against our fellow human beings, whatever the political, economic, social or religious pretext. Basic human rights are core American values. (We believe just as strongly in the need to combat other man-made scourges, such as terrorism, weapons proliferation and drug trafficking, that plague us.)

But history demonstrates that unilateral economic sanctions not only fail to address these concerns but also make heroes out of the regimes we target and impede, rather than advance, the cause of freedom in those countries.

For all of these reasons — plus the fact that U.S. economic and national security interests demand it — Congress should approve PNTR now.

Continued from p. 91

Party. Jiang's plan, spelled out in a 74-page booklet issued to party cadres, is known as "The Three Represents." [19] According to the president, the party must "always represent the development needs of China's advanced social productive forces, always represent the onward direction of China's advanced culture and always represent the fundamental interests of the largest number of Chinese people." [20]

Jiang reasons that if the party follows his simple advice of devoting itself to the Chinese people, it will prosper long into the future, regardless of economic and other changes taking place.

But many China-watchers claim that "The Three Represents" has the more immediate goal of shoring up the party's stature enough to counter any calls for a multiparty system or some milder form of political liberalization.

"They understand that they have to change if they want to stay in power," says George Washington University's Shambaugh. "They know that they have to root out corruption and become more responsive, more accountable to the people."

Indeed, by all accounts, corruption and other abuses have lowered the party's stature in the eyes of most ordinary Chinese. Protests and even violent riots are not uncommon, especially in the countryside, where poor farmers are often overtaxed by corrupt, local party officials.

Some experts say the Communists may be able to transform themselves sufficiently to retain enough popular support to hang on to power in the coming decades. "Assuming this party stays in power, it will be a very different party in 20 years," says Georgetown's Tucker. "The next generation of leaders will be more internationalist in their thinking and more open to new ideas."

But Brandeis University's Jefferson doubts that "The Three Represents" or any other efforts will restore the party's esteem in the eyes of the people. In the coming decades, he predicts, the Communists will no longer be the undisputed and sole political force in China. "The most likely scenario is that they will evolve much like South Korea or Taiwan has, in the sense that you'll see the ruling party slowly being pressured to allow more and more room for the opposition until there is a real multiparty system," Jefferson says. [21]

The Heritage Foundation's Yates sees a different path to the same outcome. "They will be incapable of changing and will lose power," he says. "I just don't think that they'll transform themselves into some sort of European-style socialist party that allows for competing voices."

The Robert F. Kennedy Center's Huang agrees: "The government will continue to crack down on its citizens and then will lose its mandate and be overthrown."

But Schmitt of the Project for the New American Century is betting that Jiang and the Communists may well hang onto power without significant political liberalization. "They're very determined not to let go, and they've learned a lesson from [Mikhail S.] Gorbachev," whose efforts to promote more political freedom led to the breakup of the Soviet Union and the fall of the Communists.

Schmitt reasons that if China's Communists continue to improve the standard of living (as they have for 20 years), they should be able to keep a lid on efforts to change the country's political system.

"Look, if [Cuban Communist leader] Fidel Castro can hang onto power for 40 years and provide little or nothing to his people," Schmitt asks, "why can't the Chinese Communists go on for decades with a growing and vibrant economy?" ■

Notes

[1] For background, see Kenneth Jost, "Taiwan, China and the U.S.," *The CQ Researcher*, May 24, 1996, pp. 457-480.

[2] For background, see Kenneth Jost, "Democracy in Asia," *The CQ Researcher*, July 24, 1998, pp. 625-648.

[3] For background, see Mary H. Cooper, "World Trade," *The CQ Researcher*, June 9, 2000, pp. 497-520.

[4] John Pomfret, "Taiwan Leader Accepts 'One China' Idea," *The Washington Post*, June 29, 2000.

[5] Quoted in Larry M. Wortzel, "Why the Administration Should Reaffirm the 'Six Assurances' to Taiwan," The Heritage Foundation, March 16, 2000.

[6] *Ibid.*

[7] Speech before the Bretton Woods Committee, a nonpartisan membership group that supports the World Bank and International Monetary Fund, May 16, 2000.

[8] Quoted in David Bonior, "Free for All," *The Washington Post*, Nov. 27, 1999.

[9] Daniel J. Boorstin, *The Discoverers* (1983), p. 192.

[10] Frederica M. Bunge and Rinn-Sup Shinn (eds.), *China: A Country Study* (1981), p. 27.

[11] *Ibid.*, pp. 27-30.

[12] *Ibid.*

[13] Harry Harding, *A Fragile Relationship: The United States and China Since 1972* (1992), pp. 216-224.

[14] For background, see David Masci, "China After Deng," *The CQ Researcher*, June 13, 1997, pp. 505-528.

[15] Karby Leggett, "China Sees a Solid Jump in Growth," *The Wall Street Journal*, July 11, 2000.

[16] *Ibid.*

[17] Cited in Dominic Ziegler, "Now Comes the Hard Part," *The Economist*, April 8, 2000.

[18] Cited in Hugo Restal, "Is China Headed for a Crash?" *The Wall Street Journal*, Sept. 2, 1999.

[19] "The Three Big Thoughts," *The Economist*, June 17, 2000.

[20] Quoted in *Ibid.*

[21] For background, see Kenneth Jost, "The Future of Korea," *The CQ Researcher*, May 19, 2000, pp. 425-448.

Bibliography

Selected Sources Used

Books

Bernstein, Richard, and Ross Munro, *The Coming Conflict with China*, Alfred A. Knopf, 1997.
Veteran journalists Bernstein and Munro argue that China and the United States are headed toward ever worsening relations and possibly war. The problem is that China wants to become the dominant power in Asia and sees America's presence in the region as the primary obstacle.

Soled, Debra E. (ed.), *China: A Nation in Transition*, CQ Press, 1995.
A writer with a special interest in Asia provides a useful introduction to China detailing its history, economy, society, and foreign policy.

Articles

"Can China Change?" *The Economist*, Oct. 2, 1999.
The article asks whether China can continue to develop economically without corresponding political changes. It concludes that if China is to become a more open society, it will almost certainly do so in spite of rather than because of the Communist Party.

Gibney, Frank, "Birth of a Superpower," *Time*, June 7, 1999.
Gibney details China's efforts to modernize its poorly equipped military.

Jost, Kenneth, "Taiwan, China and the U.S.," *The CQ Researcher*, May 24, 1996, pp. 457-480.
A slightly dated but enlightening report argues that Taiwan's surging economic self-confidence and China's increasing assertiveness pose difficult policy choices for the United States.

Lilley, James, and Arthur Waldron, "Taiwan is a 'State.' Get Over It," *The Wall Street Journal*, July 14, 1999.
Lilley and Waldron contend that treating Taiwan as a de facto independent country is the best way for China to bring about reunification.

Masci, David, "China After Deng," *The CQ Researcher*, June 13, 1997.
A report on issues facing China nearly two decades after Deng Xiaoping initiated economic reforms.

Pomfret, John, "Dissidents Back China's WTO Entry," *The Washington Post*, May 11, 2000.
Pomfret details support for China's membership in the World Trade Organization by members of the country's dissident community.

Ziegler, Dominic, "Now Comes the Hard Part," *The Economist*, April 8, 2000.
Ziegler predicts extraordinary and beneficial changes in the country's economy, but he is less certain about China's future political landscape.

Reports and Studies

Wortzel, Larry M., "Why the Administration Should Reaffirm the 'Six Assurances' to Taiwan," The Heritage Foundation, March 16, 2000.
Wortzel, director of the foundation's Asian Studies Center, argues that the United States should work harder to reassure Taiwan and stop trying to "appease" China.

FOR MORE INFORMATION

Council on Foreign Relations, 58 E. 68th St., New York, N.Y. 10021; (212) 734-0400; www.cfr.org. The nonpartisan research organization studies international issues.

Heritage Foundation, Asian Studies Center, 214 Massachusetts Ave. N.E., Washington, D.C. 20002; (202) 608-6081; www.heritage.org. Conducts research and provides information on trade, military policy and other issues that concern the United States and Asia.

Human Rights Watch, 1522 K St., N.W., Suite 910, Washington D.C. 20005; (202) 371-6592; www.hrw.org. The nonpartisan organization monitors human rights violations worldwide.

Project for the New American Century, 1150 17 St., N.W., Suite 510, Washington, D.C. 20036; (202) 293-4983. The educational organization supports American global leadership.

Robert F. Kennedy Memorial Center for Human Rights, 1367 Connecticut Ave., N.W., Suite 200, Washington, D.C. 20036; (202) 463-7575; www.rfkmemorial.org. Investigates and reports on human rights around the world.

U.S.-Asia Institute, 232 E. Capitol St., N.E., Washington, D.C. 20003; (202) 544-3181. Conducts research and sponsors overseas visits and conferences to foster greater cooperation and understanding between the United States and Asian countries.

CHINA'S OLYMPIC BID:
World Keeps Eye on Beijing;
Winning the 2008 Summer Games puts China and its Culture under a Microscope

Mike Tierney

Beijing—A beggar, sheathed in early Salvation Army, was stationed on bended knees at the entrance to the subterranean crosswalk. We dropped a green 2-yuan bill into the aluminum cup, our toll for interrupting her prayer mantra.

She identified herself as Zhao He, 62, and in our full day devoted to questioning Chinese citizens about the 2008 Olympiad, she was alone in confessing ignorance that the Games were coming to town.

We asked what this means for the homeless. "It's not good if they put us out of the city," Zhao said, a rag hiding her leathery face that nearly pressed against the pavement. She rose slightly, exposing a beeper fastened to her waist.

Nothing embodies China better than the beepin' beggar. A nation wracked with poverty and crucified because of its intolerance of basic liberties has won the Summer Olympics for its signature city, which has caught the high-tech wave of the global economy and is careening toward modernism and prosperity.

Beijing is the most controversial choice by the International Olympic Committee since Hitler's Berlin, the 1936 host. Human rights groups near and far condemned its candidacy. Amnesty International reported that, in a three-month period preceding the IOC vote, an average of nearly 20 people were executed daily for trespasses as benign as tax evasion. The European Parliament passed a resolution opposing Beijing; the U.S. House backed away only when the White House sent out signals of the president's neutrality.

The more practically minded point out that the city is so choked with pollution, your nose by day's end can be smudged by black soot. The blue sky in the promotional brochures might not be computer-generated, but most days Beijing is blanketed by a white haze.

As debate persists in other countries whether the world's most populous one deserves an Olympics, there is little dissent within its borders. An IOC survey deduced that 96 percent welcome the Games, assuring the Olympic family red-carpet treatment from the original Big Red Machine.

Our people-on-the-street interviews jibed with the committee's findings, with nary a soul (except for the wired panhandler) wishing the Games would go elsewhere. The Chinese, who at once wrestle the tag team of Inferiority Complex and No Respect, are eager to unveil the charms of a society that long has been walled off.

And, suddenly smitten by capitalism, they frame their Olympic anticipation much as Atlantans did a decade ago: an opportunity to make a few bucks—or, in this case, yuan. To the question of how you hope China most benefits from the Games came this stock response: Raise the standard of living.

Minutes after I deplaned, a hack grabbed my bag and guided me to his cab. I negotiated his original offer down to the equivalent of $30. That night, my supper hosts howled with laughter upon hearing that I paid twice the true fare.

From *The Atlanta Journal and Constitution*, September 2, 2001. Reprinted with permission.

Didn't take long for Olympic greed to strike.

"Only the supremely wise and the abysmally ignorant do not change."—*Confucius*

China, which happens to be neither, is changing at a dizzying rate, and nowhere more so than Beijing. Eight-hundred new businesses launch every day. The headgear of choice is a hard hat, what with construction engulfing the city. Cellphones are a constant companion.

Western words and ways are seeping in. English studies are mandatory at the middle-school level and offered in other grades. The Beijing mayor, as a model to his subjects, is learning the language, and we occasionally spotted someone page-turning a Chinese/English dictionary. At our hotel, employees were required to have a rudimentary grasp of English and are assigned Anglicized names.

"So many words," said Liu Shi Yao, 22, tagged Richard for reasons unclear to him. "It's difficult, but I like that."

At mall stores, "Who Let The Dogs Out" blares from speakers. Many price tags are translated into dollars. Soon, there will be no spot in the city from which a McDonald's is not visible. (At the modestly sized Malls at Oriental Plaza, we noticed three.) The 41 stops along the efficient subway, due for expansion, are announced in both tongues.

For the massive environmental makeover, a budgeted $12.2 billion will be spread among 20 projects. Motorists finally can fill up with unleaded, and industries are converting from coal to gas. Beijing factories are being disassembled, brick by brick, and moved to the outskirts.

"Absolutely remarkable achievements are being made," noted transplanted Chicagoan Emory Williams, a businessman who toots China's horn for the American Chamber of Commerce here. But the more objective say achieving fresh air and clear skies is a daunting challenge where small battles, not the war, can be won.

Nearly another $10 billion is targeted toward landscaping, neighborhood fix-up and, significantly, transportation, a saddle burr on a scale exceeding Atlanta's.

Clogged by 70,000 taxis, and with virtually all post-adolescents pedaling bicycles, the streets are chaos. Lane lines are a waste of white paint. When not frozen in traffic, drivers think nothing of turning left across five lanes of oncoming traffic, then weaving mid-speed through a phalanx of rickety, rusty two-wheelers and pedestrians.

The Chinese will batten the hatches for the expected hail of criticism.

"People will be surprised," said Mao Ji, 28, a manicurist in iron-on jeans. "They will think China is not worse than other countries."

"I have witnessed the tremendous energy of the masses. On this foundation it is possible to accomplish any task whatsoever."—*Mao Tse-Tung*

There is no task quite like staging the Summer Games. And nobody, on paper, is better suited than China. Even as the government becomes less intrusive in its subjects' lives, it still can marshal enough human resources to build or clean or secure.

Sideline pundits are prone to speculate that the IOC anointed Beijing to reward Olympic sponsors eager to spread their products and services through this largely virginal territory. Peter Franklin, director of Olympic management for Coca-Cola, said, "It's a market that has huge potential for us."

It's likely the committee was motivated more by China's potential for getting things done. Juan Antonio Samaranch's lukewarm sign-off in Atlanta was inspired as a result of headaches generated from no government authority taking charge. In China, the state calls the shots.

continues

Three years ago, Russell Probert, a Welshman, bought the restaurant-bar Frank's Place when Frank moved home to Seattle. "I think they will do a very good show," said Probert as bar stools full of Germans, Americans and Brits were turned to a Formula One race on the big screen. Prominent on a wall of license plates was a Georgia tag with the letters TOMAHAWK'N.

Probert recited a laundry list of challenges before deciding, "They can fix these—at least for a short period of time."

As Emory Williams put it, "The government will not allow China to fail. They are going to put a good face on the Olympics."

How they apply the makeup is of some concern. During its campaign in the early '90s for the 2000 Games, the government shut off electricity in certain areas to guarantee sufficient power along the route of IOC members. What appeared to be a brick home with a sloping rooftop really was all a prop made of concrete that hid a dilapidated neighborhood.

Dissidents were rounded up and lodged in insane asylums. A mentally disabled man whom the authorities thought would cast China in an unfavorable light was hauled off and allegedly killed by police.

The New York-based watchdog Human Rights in China reported that street sweeps were again rampant when 17 IOC inspectors toured in February.

Extreme measures aside, manpower is hardly a problem in a nation of 1.26 billion. Passing a construction site or entering a store, we were struck by the substantial workforce. So it will be for the Olympics, before and during. Hundreds of thousands will "volunteer," a term whose definition in China differs from ours.

"Be not afraid of going slowly, be afraid of standing still."—Chinese proverb

Bricks are being hauled to renovation areas on horse-drawn carts. If that image suggests a backward society, well, they often were zipping past traffic at a standstill.

With the Games seven years out, time is blessedly on China's side. Of the 37 sports venues, 22 are on the drawing board. Fourteen, plus the villages and media centers, will rise on the Olympic Green, undeveloped ground 3½ times the size of Central Park. These Games will approach Sydney's for their celebrated compactness. However, there is this unsettling equation: Building plus new business equals more pollution.

"The Olympics will open the window to allow the world to know more about China," said engineer Chong Yang, 34, as he sucked beer through a straw. Just make sure the window has a screen. A thin layer of dust, kicked up by power drills, seems to coat the city.

So do security forces. One unspoken selling point to the IOC was that China's ubiquitous troops will discourage all traditional forms of terrorism. At the mini-Olympic Asian Games here 10 years ago, athletes et. al. were protected by 600,000 forces. We often saw cadres of up to 20 uniformed guards marching in step down sidewalks.

With China earning honor-roll grades for its overall plan, as did Toronto and Paris, a tiebreaker was the perceived sense that the IOC owed it one. Sydney won by two votes in '93, with memories of the four-year-old Tiananmen Square massacre fresh. Though not forgotten, it has faded.

Then there is the belief that the IOC was motivated by fairness to bestow the Games on a people quite mad about fitness and athletics.

"You young people, full of vigor and vitality, are in the bloom of life, like the sun at 8 or 9 in the morning. Our hope is placed on you."—Mao Tse-Tung

The young will fulfill China's hopes with a substantial medals haul in 2008, but their parents and grandparents were part of a memorable scene I stumbled onto—one that explains why a nation emphasizing fitness has underachieved in many Olympics past.

At 6:15, just past a Sunday dawn, I plunked down 2 yuan and entered the vast Yayuantan Park. Thousands had beaten me to it.

Loose clusters of middle-aged and beyond were immersed in various forms of the meditative exercise tai chi as new-age music spilled out of boom boxes.

Old women in support hose, their purses hanging from tree knobs where branches had fallen off, smacked their wrists against each other, then slapped their ankles, thighs and buttocks. Down the path, another group was engrossed in ballroom dancing. Farther on, a fraternity of sword-thrusters, then a klatch of a dozen twirling objects with tassels hanging from them. . . .

Even with their hardships and their nicotine addiction, the Chinese strive for health. Yet, largely for cultural reasons, they have tended to shy away from sports involving head-to-head competition and so have excelled in the more artistic Olympic pursuits of gymnastics and diving.

Like everything else, that is changing. Emphasis on more sports has enabled China to climb from 11th in medals at the '88 Games in Seoul to third last year in Sydney.

Here, too, their methods have come under scrutiny. Prospective athletes are snatched at a young age and placed in resident training centers, often far from their homes. A disproportionate number of budding Olympians have failed drug tests.

China might be gaining further ground if not for the one-and-done policy. The government decree that limits families to a single child has somewhat drained the pool of young athletes.

Of those we interviewed, most plan to save their meager income for Olympic tickets—primarily swimming and soccer but also "pingpong," their nom de plume for table tennis. (And why not? The Chinese swept all four golds in Atlanta and Sydney.)

And, in spite of their supposed devotion to government, nearly all nominated an athlete such as pingponger Deng Yaping instead of a state official to light the torch at the Opening Ceremonies.

There was no vote for Wang Weilin, the brave (and vanished) soul who stood before rolling tanks at the '89 student demonstration in Tiananmen Square, a symbol for the death and destruction that taints China's image to this day.

> "If we have shortcomings, we are not afraid to have them pointed out and criticized, because we serve the people. Anyone, no matter who, may point out our shortcomings."—Mao Tse-Tung

Anyone, that is, who is Chinese. When an outsider raises the volatile issue of human rights, the locals turn defensive.

"This is a problem all over the world," said Jiao Wei Jia, 20, a student, as he posed for pictures by the Monument to the People's Heroes on Tiananmen Square. "You have racial discrimination in the U.S. We don't have that problem."

"The U.S. says it respects human rights," echoed Zhon Guang Fu, 59, an administrator, standing outside Mao's tomb, "but it's not what they say."

The standard response is that China's problems call for a tailored solution and that the West should not apply its mores.

While we might find the one-child limit repugnant, they say that population curbs prevent famine and war. "We should have family planning in accordance with the Chinese situation," said Jin Yan Hua, 22, a student.

continues

Dou Li Guo, a farmer, chooses one of his crops for a different-strokes metaphor. "In the U.S.," said Dou, 27, "you like to eat bread. We like rice."

Dou hails from the northeast, home base of Li Hongzhi, the lightning-rod leader of the outlawed Falun Gong spiritual movement. Dou applauds its banishment, labeling followers heretics and Li a cheat. He says political demonstrations offer no solutions, so why even allow them?

"China," he concluded, "is not as bad as you imagine."

This was a nation where, within the last half-century, cannibalism was practiced. Where, a decade ago, hugging and kissing was prohibited at Beijing University. Where organs allegedly are harvested from just-executed criminals for sale to the rich or influential. Where members of Falun Gong are arrested and imprisoned, as a TV editor named Joyce (the only interviewee who declined to disclose her last name) witnessed in April when two women unfurled a banner and were whisked away. Where the pop star Chang Hui-Mei is banned because she sang at the inauguration of Taiwan's president. Where, if you believe Human Rights in China, as many as 800 repatriation camps hold more than 2 million people—20 percent under 16, none charged with a specific crime.

And where media gets hassled. As we completed one interview on the Square, a guard approached and angrily asked us to identify ourselves and our newspaper—and to specify what questions we asked. We complied with the first two requests, not the third.

"Those who say it cannot be done should not interrupt the person doing it."—Chinese proverb

For the next seven years, the 515,000-yuan ($64,000) question is: Will the spotlight now shining on China compel it to extend liberties and mind its manners, or will it consider winning the host role as legitimizing its old ways?

History has no clear answer. Hitler marched into the Rhineland and Brezhnev invaded Afghanistan one year before their nations held the Games. Yet, in South Korea, parliamentary democracy, constitution reforms and a reduction in police surveillance of political candidates preceded the '88 Olympics.

From afar, the world will keep an eye on more than the construction crews at work. Will the rate of executions decline? Will political protest be tolerated? Will the massive amounts of funds diverted toward Games preparations deny citizens their basic needs and drive them deeper into poverty?

I thought about a trickle-down effect for the masses when a boy, maybe 5, stalked me for an entire block, clutching my wrists, folding his hands in a prayer sign and repeating what I assumed to be, "Spare change, mister?"

If nothing else, the winning bid brought smiles to a people unaccustomed to showing off their molars. On July 13, when Samaranch announced, "It's Beijing," the parties lasted until sunup.

At the IOC meetings in Moscow, officials picked up George Hirthler of Helikon Media, an Atlanta firm that advised China during its campaign, and twirled him around. "I don't think I've seen anybody so proud," Hirthler said.

The Chinese do care about what others think. They told us the world should know that they are kind, warm-hearted, caring and hospitable. And that there is ample room for improvement.

"Through this, we can get wiser," said Joyce, the editor with no surname. "The Olympics can bring some fresh air here."

China Trade Bill Remains Intact as Senate Rejects Arms Sanctions

By Chuck McCutcheon with Lori Nitschke

With the surprisingly resounding rejection of a proposal aimed at checking China's national security threat to the United States, the Senate is poised to overwhelmingly approve legislation Sept. 19 that would establish permanent normal trade relations with China.

At least 70 senators are expected to vote to clear the bill (HR 4444), a final vote of confidence for an initiative that has been at the center of one of the most hard-fought lobbying campaigns in recent years.

By making permanent China's standing as a normal U.S. trading partner, the measure would seal a sweeping agreement under which the world's most populous nation will open its markets to American goods and services. The prospect of those benefits led the Clinton administration to team up with the business community against unions, environmentalists, human right advocates and defense hawks, who maintain that some of China's behavior might be worsened given the reward of a trade deal.

The White House and business lobby successfully opposed all amendments to address those concerns, out of fear that altering the measure and forcing its return to the House could doom it so late in the 106th Congress. The House passed the bill in May.

Proponents heaved a huge sigh of relief Sept. 13 after the defeat of the marquee amendment—a move by Sens. Fred Thompson, R-Tenn., and Robert G. Torricelli, D-N.J., to impose sanctions on Chinese companies if they were caught exporting nuclear, chemical or biological weapons. Buffeted by procedural setbacks and bipartisan criticism, their amendment was tabled, or killed, 65–32.

"I was hoping we could get into the 40s rather than the 30s," Thompson said afterward, tacitly acknowledging that his proposal never posed a true threat to the China bill. "Clearly, the no-amendment strategy is working for them."

Torricelli agreed: "The pressure from the White House and business community was intense and could not be resisted."

Several Republicans who had endorsed the proposal voted to table the amendment because, they said, it did not belong in the trade bill. Max Baucus, D-Mont., a leading proponent of the China bill, attributed the amendment's large margin of defeat to the realization of about a dozen senators that the measure "probably caused more problems than it was going to solve."

Supporters of enhanced trade with China professed not to be bothered by the Senate's prolonged deliberations on the bill, which stretched over 10 days. Some, however, expressed frustration with Majority Leader Trent Lott, R-Miss., for waiting so long to move on a bill that so many senators would seek to amend.

"A major tactical error," said Rep. Robert T. Matsui, D-Calif., the administration's point man on the measure. "A bill like that should never be brought up in the last month of Congress."

Others faulted Lott for allowing consideration of amendments they said could send the wrong signal internationally were they adopted, or wondered if his tactics were designed to gain leverage on year-end negotiations with the president on other issues.

"I don't understand the strategy or the position of Sen. Lott on this," said Joseph R. Biden Jr. of Delaware, the Foreign Relations Committee's ranking Democrat. "At this point, to turn down China has enormous foreign policy consequences, as far as I'm concerned."

From *CQ Weekly,* Sept. 16, 2000.

Lott offered no apologies for his handling of the trade issue. He noted that he supported efforts in July to offer an earlier version of the Thompson-Torricelli proposal (S·2645) to the fiscal 2001 intelligence authorization bill (S 2507), but that he was met with objections from Democrats.

Lott was among the 23 Republicans who joined nine Democrats in supporting the amendment.

Security vs. Commerce

The failure of the Thompson-Torricelli amendment underscored how difficult it has been for Republicans worried about China's danger to U.S. national security to make their voices heard over those more concerned with promoting commerce. Although senior GOP lawmakers have condemned the administration for using the term "strategic partnership" to characterize U.S.-Chinese relations, they also have heeded the warning of the party's business allies not to stir up any anti-China sentiment.

Thompson pointed to recent intelligence reports of increasing Chinese export of weapons of mass destruction as evidence Congress should hold the government in Beijing accountable.

The amendment, as weakened in recent weeks in an effort to draw more support, would have required the president to review China's proliferation activities each year and cut off technology exports as well as government loans and credits if he determined any weapons or components were leaving the country. The president would have been allowed to waive the sanctions in the name of national security.

Opponents questioned whether unilateral sanctions would prove effective against China and said few other nations were likely to follow the U.S. lead in punishing the country, so the effect could be to put American companies at a competitive disadvantage.

Even before the amendment was defeated, Thompson vowed to continue working on the issue. Other supporters of reining in proliferation welcomed having more time. "It needs to be modified, it needs to be debated, the Commerce, State and Defense departments need to weigh in, industry needs to weigh in," said Larry M. Wortzel, director of the Asian Studies Center at the Heritage Foundation, a conservative think tank.

Coincidentally, the vote came the same day that former Los Alamos National Laboratory scientist Wen Ho Lee was freed after striking a deal with federal prosecutors to plead guilty to a single felony charge in the 59-count indictment against him. Lee's release was an embarrassing setback for the Clinton administration, which had accused the Taiwan-born physicist of giving highly sensitive nuclear secrets to China.

Republicans have sought to make a political issue of Chinese espionage. In the Senate alone, five committees have held more than 20 hearings on the subject, and angry GOP senators promised more hearings on the Justice Department's handling of the Lee case.

Democrats, however, said Republicans did not acknowledge the possibility that congressional overreaction played any role in shaping events on the case. They said the GOP misplayed its hand by appearing so partisan on China. "Whether it is trade, whether it is human rights, whether it is the environment, whether it is Wen Ho Lee, there's a legitimate cause to look at all these things," Biden said. "I'm of the opinion they were looked at through the prism of politics at the front end. It was viewed through the wrong prism."

Other Amendments

The Senate rebuffed 17 other amendments, all primarily on the grounds that their inclusion could delay or perhaps destroy the measure's chances for enactment. Among them were proposals:

By Jesse Helms, R-N.C., to require the president to certify that China had made strides on improving a range of human rights issues, including dismantling labor camps, opening access to Tibet and reviewing prison sentences and releasing those imprisoned for religious or political reasons. Defeated 32–63 on Sept. 12.

By Robert C. Smith, R-N.H., who offered three proposals to require the congressional-executive branch commission created under the bill to monitor China's cooperation with U.S. goals on human rights issues, such as reducing the harvesting of organs from prisoners. That one was defeated, 29–66, on Sept. 13.

By Paul Wellstone, D-Minn., to require the president to certify that China is not exporting goods made with prison labor before he grants the country permanent normal trade status. Defeated, 29–68, on Sept. 12.

By Robert C. Byrd, D-W.Va., to require that China disclose information on how it will reduce reliance on state-owned businesses and other government intervention in commerce. Defeated by voice vote Sept. 12.

By Helms, to require the Commerce secretary to establish a voluntary code of conduct for U.S. businesses operating in China. Defeated, 23–73, on Sept. 13.

By Ernest F. Hollings, D-S.C., to restrict eligibility for assistance from the Export-Import Bank or Overseas Private Investment Corp. to those with no recent advanced technology transfers to China or to those who had not recently moved production plants to China. Defeated by voice vote Sept. 14.

After the China Bill: Fresh Start for the Trade Expansion Debate

By Lori Nitschke

The overwhelming Senate vote to make permanent China's standing as a normal trading partner of the United States is more than a historic milestone in Sino-American relations and the finale in one of the most consequential debates of the 106th Congress. It also is a dramatic illustration of the breadth of support that trade expansion is capable of generating.

The 83–15 vote on Sept. 19 to clear the China trade legislation (HR 4444) is no guarantee, however, that the next Congress and the next president will face easy sledding when it comes to trade expansion.

The questions on their collective trade plate during the next two years are wide-ranging: Whether to revive an expedited process for congressional debate of trade pacts; whether to embrace a bilateral trade deal with Vietnam reached this summer and another one about to be sealed with Jordan; what weight to give attempts to chip away at sanctions on countries unfriendly to the United States, especially Cuba and Iran; and how to tackle public concerns about international commerce, namely its effects on labor rights and environmental degradation.

Outside Congress, U.S. negotiators will continue to push trade expansion forward, by attempting to reduce trade barriers world-wide through the World Trade Organization (WTO) and trying to facilitate trade throughout the Western Hemisphere.

Debates on the benefits of most of those actions will not be as easy to sell to Congress—and the public—as the virtues of enhanced and stable trade with the world's most populous nation. The sales pitch for that bill was eased by the sheer number of cuts to tariffs, quotas and other trade barriers that the Chinese committed to make last fall in return for one change to U.S. law: ending the annual rite of the president and Congress reviewing China's behavior before granting its imports another year of low tariffs.

The bill's enactment promises that billions of dollars in economic benefits will come to American business. They will come despite continued complaints that a country with a poor labor and human rights history is not worthy of the same low-tariff treatment most other countries get. Still, the issue has received scant debate outside Washington or on the campaign trail.

Both Vice President Al Gore, the Democratic nominee, and Gov. George W. Bush of Texas, the Republican nominee, supported the bill. Both also espouse the importance of continuing the expansion of trade—particularly within the Western Hemisphere—that has been one of the foreign policy hallmarks of the Clinton administration.

The candidates' similar views, and the splits trade creates in both major political parties, has forced trade expansion into the background on the campaign trail. When it does come up, it is usually in the stump speeches of the two most prominent minor party candidates—Reform nominee Pat Buchanan and Green nominee Ralph Nader. Although from the right and left edges of the American political spectrum, they share an opposition to trade expansion, contending that it is wrong to give potential boosts to corporate profits priority over national security, in Buchanan's view, or the well-being of people worldwide, in Nader's.

A similar political pattern was evident in the Senate's vote Sept. 19, in which the smaller-than-expected minority was formed by five of the more liberal Democrats, five of the most conservative

From *CQ Weekly*, Sept. 23, 2000.

Republicans, three GOP senators with pro-union leanings and two Democrats from import sensitive states in voting against the bill. (The Senate's 83 percent show of support dwarfed the 54 percent House majority that passed the bill May 24.)

Fast track authority

If either Bush or Gore is to achieve his goal of expanding trade, the path would be eased by the renewal of "fast track" trade negotiating authority, granted to each president since Gerald R. Ford but allowed to lapse at the end of 1994. The procedure allows the administration to negotiate a trade agreement without fear that Congress will amend the pact. Instead, when a president submits a bill to Congress to implement a trade agreement, Congress has 90 days to endorse it or reject it, but may not alter it.

Two years ago, the House defeated Clinton's request to revive this procedure.

The next president will be under great pressure, particularly if Democrats control all or part of Congress, to alter the fast track procedure of the past to ensure that trade's effects on laborers' rights and environmental degradation are taken into account.

That debate could be joined on some trade agreements that will be put before the 107th Congress, including those with Vietnam and Jordan. The pending deal with Jordan will contain language on labor and the environment, according to U.S. Trade Representative Charlene Barshefsky, and could serve as a test case for tackling such concerns overall.

Bush would likely seek to revive the previous fast track terms, and would probably get his wish if Republicans retain control of Congress. If Democrats take back the House their insistence on addressing labor and environmental matters could polarize the debate anew, straining trade's long-standing tradition—so clearly echoed in the Senate vote—of being a non-partisan issue.

Gore has already said that if elected he would ensure that future trade pacts address labor rights and environmental quality. How strongly he would push would be paramount to his success in winning concessions in those areas, on which many nations say the United States has no business butting in. So his promise could bog down progress on trade expansion.

It is also not clear that Gore would seek to revive fast track. Barshefsky, in a Sept. 20 interview, said that Congress' growing involvement in trade matters may make the need for fast track obsolete.

"We need to think very carefully about whether to pursue fast track," said Barshefsky, whose views are likely to carry weight even though she is unlikely to be a part of a Gore administration. "The question has to be considered anew in a very dispassionate way and not blinded by old thinking."

Scaling the Great Wall

Those on both sides of the trade debate agree on one thing: Making permanent the U.S. trade relationship with China—and making possible billions of dollars in projected benefits for U.S. industries—was a much easier sell than a somewhat fuzzy trade procedure such as fast track will be.

As part of its effort to join the WTO later this year, China committed in November to significant cuts in tariffs and other trade barriers on U.S.-made products. The United States has similarly cut tariffs on Chinese-made products since 1980, a year after leaders in Beijing signed a trade pact with President Jimmy Carter. Since 1989, Congress has annually voted to uphold that trade status.

Big business poured millions into lobbying for a permanent trade relationship with China, and smaller organizations, such as farm groups, put grass-roots pressure on lawmakers. The high-technology industry cut its fledgling lobbying teeth on the bill.

continues

Enactment of the bill had also been one of the few top-tier priorities for Clinton during his last year in the White House. His signature will provide the coda on a presidency that will be marked as one under which international trade was greatly expanded. He opened his first term by pushing through a hesitant Congress the North American Free Trade Agreement (PL 103-182), which had been negotiated by his predecessor, George Bush. The next year, just before his fast-track power lapsed, he pushed Congress to send him a measure (PL 103-465) to implement a new General Agreement on Tariffs and Trade, the sweeping changes to the world trade system under which the WTO was created.

"The China debate became a debate on the overall course of the China relationship," said Myron A. Brilliant, a lobbyist for the U.S. Chamber of Commerce, which has led lobbying campaigns for trade expansion. "On trade agreements and on fast track, it centers much more on the role of labor and environmental issues."

Daniel A. Seligman, director of the Sierra Club's Responsible Trade Campaign, said that "if the debate is around a country, the issue often gets reduced to whether or not you like that particular country. Having a debate around a trade agreement or trade negotiating authority, then it's easier to conduct the debate on a level of principle."

The principles Seligman would like debated focus on preventing world trade rules from tying the hands of governments that want to set their own environmental and labor laws. Environmentalists say that in the name of creating a level playing field for businesses, the WTO has essentially overridden local regulations.

Some in Congress see the China debate as an example of how they might deal with some constituent worries about the global marketplace.

Despite months of ardent lobbying, success for the China bill was not assured until a week before the House vote, when its supporters agreed to add on creation of an executive branch-congressional commission to review China's record on labor and human rights, the environment and other issues. Any legislation it recommended would receive expedited consideration in Congress.

"If fast track did take into consideration those issues on the same basis the China trade bill does, it would be a worthy compromise," Charles E. Grassley, R-Iowa, chairman of the Senate Finance International Trade Subcommittee, told reporters Sept. 19.

"In my judgment, there's no choice but to tackle these issues; they won't go away," said Rep. Sander M. Levin, D-Mich., a sponsor of the additional language, which has been derided by unions and other opponents of the China bill as no more than a "fig leaf" to cover Congress' failure to take steps guaranteeing that the Chinese will see their lives improved along with expanded trade.

Some pro-trade Democrats such as Rep. Robert T. Matsui of California, who led the administration's campaign for passage of the China bill, say it will be necessary in future deals to take such steps. Without them, said Rep. Sherrod Brown, D-Ohio, a leading opponent of recent trade expansion legislation, fast track will remain a dead letter. "If Bill Clinton couldn't do it . . . no president will be able to do it," he said in an interview Sept. 19.

Some of the most pro-trade members in both parties, however, see such steps as unnecessary. Congress would "build the support we need for fast track," Sen. Phil Gramm, R-Texas, said in an interview Sept. 19, if there was "a president that we trust." Former Rep. David K. McCurdy, D-Okla., (1981–95), president of the pro-trade Electronics Industries Alliance, said, "There's no reason to qualify it [fast track] right now."

The Long Term

For the loose coalition of environmental, labor, religious, consumer and other groups that lost the hard-fought battle over China trade, the last year has still presented some bright spots. They pressed their cause to the forefront of national awareness with their protests at the WTO session in Seattle last year, and they see the lingering attention as offering hope for future success.

While she termed the China loss "a pretty big blow," Thea Lee, the AFL-CIO's assistant director of public policy, said that "there's a long-term struggle that we have made progress on."

Seligman was less circumspect. "I think Seattle knocked Humpty Dumpty off the wall in a way that the victory on China will not be able to put him back together," he said.

While some believe the China vote showed that the anti-globalization forces are not as strong as thought, it is increasingly unlikely that Seligman's group and others will be shut out of the arenas in which trade policy is made.

Much of their focus in coming years will not be on Congress. A dialogue with the nations of Latin America, initiated in the Reagan and Bush administrations and known as the Free Trade Area of the Americas, is considered a prime spot to address trade's affects on environment and culture. The talks have a 2005 deadline, although Barshefsky said a new president could speed their conclusion. While Congress would not have a vote on the process until a trade agreement was completed, members have provided input to U.S. negotiators and are expected to be consulted more often as the process zeroes in on controversial issues.

This proposal would essentially extend NAFTA throughout the Western Hemisphere, but the next president may aim to give some nations a head start. For instance, GOP nominee Bush's father promised to work for Chile's inclusion in 1992. (The Clinton administration has done little to advance that proposal.) In addition, some Republicans, such as Gramm, want to see Great Britain admitted to NAFTA. And members will also push for a one-year exemption from some textile quotas for Colombia, Ecuador, Peru and Bolivia, if that proposal does not find its way into an end-of-the-session bill this year.

Separate negotiations will also probably be ongoing within the WTO on a new round of talks to reduce trade barriers across a spectrum of industries.

Although the Seattle meeting failed to launch a new round as had been anticipated, some observers believe the election of a new U.S. president may jump start world-wide trade talks. Such discussions usually take three to five years to be completed.

Because Clinton, as a lame duck, could not see through any negotiations he launched, his status has been an obstacle to beginning new trade projects. Many in Congress look forward to returning to full strength next year.

"It may be on the back burner in the campaign—all foreign policy issues seem to be—but it will very much be on the front burner" in 2001, Levin said.

Trade with China: The Next Steps

Lori Nitschke

Q: What will happen under the bill the Senate cleared Sept. 19?

A: The measure (HR 4444) would allow the president to permanently extend normal, non-discriminatory treatment to Chinese goods once China is accepted into the World Trade Organization (WTO). It would do this by permanently exempting China from the requirements of the Jackson-Vanik amendment to the 1974 Trade Act (93-618). Under that law, this normal trade relations status—known as NTR—may be extended to some countries for only one year at a time. The law was designed to punish communist nations that made it difficult for citizens to leave.

Q: How will this enhance trade between the United States and China?

A: Before permanent NTR for China may take effect, the president must certify to Congress that the terms for China's entry into the WTO are as rigorous as those agreed to under a bilateral trade agreement signed Nov. 15 by U.S. Trade Representative Charlene Barshefsky and Chinese Premier Zhu Rongji. In that deal, Beijing promised to phase out its import quotas and make steep cuts during the next four years in its tariffs on U.S.-made goods.

Q: What is the WTO, and who belongs to it?

A: The Geneva-based body governs world trade, ruling on disputes between countries and otherwise monitoring international commerce. It was created as part of the Uruguay Round of the General Agreement on Tariffs and Trade, which Congress agreed to implement through a law (PL 103-465) enacted six years ago. Albania became the 138th member on Sept. 8. China is among 30 other nations that are attempting to join. Another such nation is Vietnam; as with China, its push to join the WTO was enhanced when it signed a trade agreement with the United States. That pact was reached in July.

Q: What else must China do before it may join the WTO?

A: The world's most populous nation still must firm up negotiations with the WTO over the protocol for its membership. This will focus largely on deadlines for implementing changes in China required by WTO rules, such as moving away from state ownership of industries. Finalization of this language and of the details of trade agreements with any other WTO members will probably come either late this year or early next year.

Q: What other countries are likely to join the WTO, and how will Congress be involved?

A: Taiwan has been waiting for years to join and is expected to be allowed in the WTO shortly after China. Although China considers Taiwan a renegade province, U.S. leaders believe that will not prevent Taiwan from joining. Russia is the next major country likely to join, or accede. While officials there have recently announced their intent to speed the process of winning membership, it looks to be years away. Russia does not have permanent NTR, which means Congress would have to take a vote on Russia's trade status, such as it just has on China. But if the United States were to sign a trade agreement with Russia, which would be a likely precursor to WTO membership, Congress would have a vote on that if it changed any U.S. laws.

Q: What other nations have an irregular trade relationship with the United States ?

A: Seven countries do not have any form of NTR: Afghanistan, Cuba, Laos, North Korea, Vietnam, Serbia and Montenegro. President Clinton has waived Vietnam's compliance with Jackson-Vanik, but

From *CQ Weekly*, Sept. 23, 2000.

the country still needs its trade pact approved by Congress to be eligible for normal trade status. Thirteen other nations have NTR conditionally, so long as they allow free emigration. Clinton has certified every six months that Russia and 10 other former states of the Soviet Union—Armenia, Azerbaijan, Georgia, Kazakhstan, Kyrgyzstan, Moldova, Russia, Tajikistan, Turkmenistan, Ukraine and Uzbekistan—along with Albania are complying fully with Jackson-Vanik. He has granted a waiver of Jackson-Vanik requirements to the former Soviet republic of Belarus.

2000 Legislative Summary: China's Trade Status
Bill: HR 4444—PL 106-286

Status: Business leaders, particularly those in the high-tech and agriculture sectors, helped push a skeptical House and a generally gridlocked Senate to pass legislation to permanently apply the same low tariff rates to Chinese imports as those already applied to goods from all but a handful of countries. President Clinton made the bill a top priority during his final year in office. Enactment capped his efforts to expand trade opportunities for U.S. businesses that began in 1993 with the enactment of a law (PL 103-182) to implement the North American Free Trade Agreement (NAFTA). The measure also put the U.S. imprimatur on China's bid to join the World Trade Organization (WTO), the body that governs global commerce.

Synopsis: Goods from China had won reduced tariff rates annually since 1980, after President Jimmy Carter re-established trade ties with Beijing. Under the Jackson-Vanik amendment to the 1974 Trade Act (PL 93-618), the president was required to annually review the trade status of certain communist nations such as China.

China's efforts to join the WTO conflicted with that law. WTO rules require member nations to grant one another's products "permanent normal trade relations status," unless they are willing to forgo the benefits of more open trade with a particular country.

In November 1999, U.S. Trade Representative Charlene Barshefsky and Chinese Premier Zhu Rongji reached an agreement to drastically cut tariffs, quotas and other trade barriers on U.S. exports to China. In return, the administration agreed to support China's entry into the WTO.

That required Congress to vote to remove China from the list of communist countries subject to Jackson-Vanik. The administration knew the issue would embolden opponents of close U.S.-China trade relations, such as labor unions and environmental groups, and critics of China's social policies, including human rights activists and social conservatives, at a particularly uncomfortable time for Democrats. Facing their best chance in six years to retake the House, Democrats were wary of embracing the China bill and, thereby, offending the very constituencies they were courting in the campaign.

As a result, the White House approached the issue gingerly at first. Republicans pressured the president to become more involved in the fight, as he had done with NAFTA. In March, Clinton submitted his formal proposal to Congress, which became the heart of the bill that was debated. The submission prompted the onset of one of the most intense lobbying campaigns of the 106th Congress. House Minority Whip David E. Bonior, D-Mich., led the opposition and predicted the vote would be close enough that one or two members could make the difference. At the same time, business leaders initiated a multimillion-dollar advertising campaign.

A few House centrists began to look for an option other than "yes" or "no." Sander M. Levin, D-Mich., and Doug Bereuter, R-Neb., explored ways to hold China accountable for its actions on human rights, compliance with trade rules and other issues. As the vote drew near, they came together with a proposal to establish a joint congressional-executive branch commission to monitor China's actions and report to Congress. When GOP leaders agreed to attach the plan to the China bill, their success was assured. Whips said the Levin-Bereuter package had won over as many as 30 votes. The China bill passed by a 40-vote margin.

From *CQ Weekly*, December 16, 2000.

Passage by the more internationalist Senate was never in doubt, and both sides expected an expeditious vote there. But Fred Thompson, R-Tenn., and Robert G. Torricelli, D-N.J., pressed leaders to allow a vote on their proposal to require the president to impose sanctions if China was found to be contributing to the spread of weapons of mass destruction. Their proposal, popular with many conservatives, threatened to force the bill back to the House if it was attached to the measure. Majority Leader Trent Lott, R-Miss., took four months to bring the bill to the floor. When he did, senators agreed, 65–32, to kill the Thompson-Torricelli amendment, and voted overwhelmingly to clear the bill.

Legislative action: House passed HR 4444 (H Rept 106-632), 237–197, on May 24.

Senate cleared HR 4444, 83–15, on Sept. 19.

President signed the bill Oct. 10.

Index